August 1914

August 1914

France, the Great War, and a Month That Changed the World Forever

BRUNO CABANES

Translated by Stephanie O'Hara

Yale
UNIVERSITY PRESS
New Haven and London

Published with assistance from the Kingsley Trust Association Publication Fund
established by the Scroll and Key Society of Yale College.

English translation © 2016 by Yale University. Translated 2016 by Stephanie
O'Hara.
Originally published as *Août 14*. © Éditions GALLIMARD, Paris, 2014.
Map by Bill Nelson.

All rights reserved.
This book may not be reproduced, in whole or in part, including illustrations,
in any form (beyond that copying permitted by Sections 107 and 108 of the U.S.
Copyright Law and except by reviewers for the public press), without written
permission from the publishers.

Yale University Press books may be purchased in quantity for educational,
business, or promotional use. For information, please e-mail sales.press@yale.
edu (U.S. office) or sales@yaleup.co.uk (U.K. office).

Set in Janson Roman type by IDS Infotech, Ltd.
Printed in the United States of America.

Library of Congress Control Number: 2015959532
ISBN 978-0-300-20827-6 (hardcover : alk. paper)

A catalogue record for this book is available from the British Library.

This paper meets the requirements of ANSI/NISO Z39.48-1992 (Permanence
of Paper).

10 9 8 7 6 5 4 3 2 1

Contents

CONTENTS

Acknowledgments

My thanks go to Stéphane Audoin-Rouzeau, Annette Becker, David Blight, Raphaëlle Branche, Anne and Bernard Chambaz, Élodie and Jérôme Chapuis, Alice Conklin, Maïa and Thomas Dodman, Theodora Dragostinova and Bud Barnes, Valérie Hannin, John Horne, Christian Ingrao, Brian Jordan, Anne and Neil Josephy-Zack, Alice Kaplan, Gina and Doug Lee, Patricia Martin, Hervé Mazurel, Carol and John Merriman, Séverine Nikel, Geoffrey Parker, Antoine Prost, Mary Louise Roberts, Anne and Benoît Rolland, Henry Rousso, Véronique and Vincent Roux, Maurie Samuels, Jennifer Siegel, Leonard V. Smith, Gene Tempest, and Francesca Trivellato for their friendship, advice, and support. Twenty-five years ago, I began to work on the First World War with Jean-Jacques Becker, the great historian of 1914. I owe him so much.

My family and I are grateful for the warm welcome we found in Columbus and Bexley after arriving from

Connecticut in 2014. I owe a great deal to my wonderful friends and colleagues from the History Department at Ohio State University, to Peter Hahn and Nate Rosenstein, and especially to my colleagues in military history, Mark Grimsley, Joe Guilmartin, Pete Mansoor, Geoffrey Parker, and Jennifer Siegel. It is a great honor to be the inaugural Donald G. and Mary A. Dunn Chair in Modern Military History. I wish to express my profound gratitude to Donald Dunn and the Dunn family for their kindness, their support, and their generosity. I cannot imagine my life without the pleasure of teaching and the intellectual company of students. I am particularly grateful to our many talented graduate students at Ohio State University.

I thank my editor at Gallimard, Ran Halévi, for everything this book owes to him, and also Arnaud Jamin and Philippe Bernier. At Yale University Press, I had the privilege of working with Eric Brandt, Chris Rogers, Erica Hanson, and Dan Heaton. Thanks must be extended to the readers for the Press who provided me with helpful advice. For having read and commented on my manuscript at various stages, my dear friends Alice Kaplan and Bernard Chambaz have my profound gratitude. Special thanks also to Stephanie O'Hara, associate professor at the University of Massachusetts Dartmouth, for her splendid translation of my book.

Gene Tempest shared her knowledge of the environmental history of the war. Damien Baldin, Emmanuel Saint-Fuscien, and Clémentine Vidal-Naquet provided documents, advice, and bibliographic references. Many thanks to them, and to Emmanuel Dupont, Mattie Fitch, Anthony Guiet, and especially Michel Roux and Pierre Simon, who did significant archival research. I also wish to thank the staffs of the Archives départementales in the Bouches-du-Rhône, Loire-Atlantique, Maine-et-Loire, Mayenne, Puy-de-Dôme, and Vendée, as well as the staffs of the Archives nationales, the Archives de la préfecture de police de Paris, the Bibliothèque de documentation internationale contemporaine in Nanterre, and the Sterling Library at Yale University, all of whom provided access to their marvelous collections.

For more than ten years, my wife, Flora, and I have been living in the United States. Without her love, support, and endless generosity, nothing would be possible. More profoundly than I can express, she has made me see what really matters in life.

This book is dedicated to our beautiful daughters. Gabrielle and Constance, this book is for you, with all my love, in memory of your great-grand-uncle Athanase, whose name means "the immortal": a particularly fitting name for a survivor of the collective catastrophe of 1914. "I would rather never have been born," he used to say, "than have to relive everything I went through."

Bexley, October 2015

Translator's Acknowledgments

Sincere thanks to Edward M. Strauss, translator of *Poilu: The World War I Notebooks of Corporal Louis Barthas, Barrelmaker, 1914–1918* (Yale University Press, 2014), and to an anonymous reader for their patience and helpful comments on the manuscript. It has been a pleasure to work with the extremely efficient and accommodating Erica Hanson and Dan Heaton of Yale University Press. Jesse Waidler of the Massachusetts Army National Guard kindly discussed military terminology with me. My colleague Marie McDonough provided invaluable assistance in translating Chapters 6, 7, and 8. And finally, I thank Bruno Cabanes for his unstinting support and collegiality.

Introduction

On August 1, 1914, war erupted into the lives of millions of men and women across France. Men set out to fight, confident that their cause was just. Plan XVII, adopted in April 1913, gave hopes for a swift victory. The joint forces of the French army prepared for combat; their mission was to strike the center of the German front. It was thought that the end of the conflict would be settled in one battle, perhaps costly in terms of human lives, but decisive. With hindsight, after four years of bloody, murderous combat that traumatized an entire generation, it is astonishing that the Great War was initially conceived of as an affair of a few weeks.

In fact, this was very nearly what happened—but not following the scenario that French strategists imagined. Only three weeks after the mobilization, thousands upon thousands of young men were slaughtered on the battlefields of Charleroi, Rossignol, and Morhange. Retreat followed at the end of August. This early catastrophe left an indelible imprint on French soldiers and civilians alike. Had it not been for the counteroffensive on the Marne at the beginning of September, the war on the Western Front might have ended there, inflicting an even more humiliating defeat on the French than had the Franco-Prussian War of 1870–71.

Intense violence characterized the early weeks of the First World War. The decisive month of August 1914 has often been studied from the viewpoint of diplomats and general staffs but rarely from the perspective of a country and its inhabitants in the grip of war. This book, then, is first of all a history of the French as they faced one of the most frightening collective ordeals of the twentieth century. It is also a history of rural France, whose everyday life in 1914 to 1918 remains largely unknown. Yet it was this France that supplied half of the mobilized soldiers. And this is a history of urban France, which saw thousands of soldiers stream in and out of its train stations. In short, this book is an intimate history of the end of a world.

Through largely neglected sources such as eyewitness accounts, préfets' reports, police notes, personal correspondence, and diaries, I seek to bring back to life the passions, hopes, and illusions that historians often forget: the pain of separation and the anguish over what is to come; the fear of the enemy within; the threat of invasion. My previous books focused on the transition from war to peace and the long shadows of war. Here I take the opposite approach, examining how individuals and communities grappled with a quick transition from peace to war, and the spectrum of feelings and impressions this produced.[1] To leave for the front is both exalting and traumatizing, incommensurate with the collective emotions of peacetime. Patriotic fervor, carefully staged, silences the pacifists among the undecided. Families separate, and the family unit is reorganized. Relationships between men and women, between old and young, are altered. War brings with it a new relationship to time and space. Civilians live their lives to the rhythm of official communiqués; they wait for letters and worry about their loved ones at the front. Endless troop transports move across the country and reshape its territory. Floods of refugees flee invasion, spreading rumors that amplify still more the ordeal of war.

Fall 1914 is generally thought to be the first turning point of the Great War. This was when trench warfare replaced the war of movement. In fact, it took only several days, several weeks at most, for France to fully experience the reality of modern war. As soon as hostilities started, the citizens of enemy countries who were living in France suffered reprisals but found themselves unable to flee, due to the closing of the borders. German and Austrian civilians (or those thought to be) were attacked or sent to internment camps. They became scapegoats in a war without restraint. Even more cruel was the fate of those whose family names or accents marked them out as foreigners in their own country: immigrants who had been in France for a long time; French Jews, victims of a resurgence of anti-Semitism; former refugees from Alsace-Lorraine mistaken for Germans. In the tumult of the mobilization, at the very heart of an apparently peaceful society, demonization of the enemy within broke out.

In those regions that had been invaded, the basic distinction that humanitarian law made between combatants and civilians was abolished out of hand. Some six thousand Belgian and French civilians were summarily executed in less than two months. In the regions held by the Germans, a harsh policy of occupation was put in place by the end of the summer. It abolished individual freedoms and transformed the population into a submissive workforce. On the battlefields, the eruption of violence was just as brutal. A generation that had grown up with the distant memory of the war of 1870–71 suddenly faced the ordeal of shells and machine guns.

For all these men in the flower of their youth, the month of August 1914 was an initiation not just into the harshness of military life but into war in all its inhumanity. Meanwhile, the rest of society went into mourning. Many families had no bodies to bury; soldiers had died pulverized by shells, or their corpses had been abandoned at the moment of retreat. In our collective memory, the catastrophes of Verdun and the Somme in 1916 have eclipsed the unprecedented violence of the war's first month. I have sought to recapture this violence here.

This was a collective catastrophe as well as an individual one, a catastrophe on the scale of an entire society and on the smaller scale of family life. An entire world disappeared amid the fracas of the war's outbreak. By August 1914, it was felt, it was *known*, that nothing would ever be the same again. In one of his accounts of the war, the future novelist Maurice Genevoix described how he heard the news of the mobilization: he was spending the summer in his small hometown of Châteauneuf-sur-Loire, far from Paris and his fellow students at the École normale supérieure. Accompanied by a young cousin, he started to climb the bell tower that overlooked the marketplace. Then the tocsin began to ring out. Shaken, he descended at once. The sight of the market, which met his eyes as he left the church, underscored for him the fragility of a world struck by war. Nothing seemed to have changed; the marketgoers left, after making their last purchases. And yet nothing was the same anymore. The church bells of this little town on the banks of the Loire "were tolling for the end of the world, for thousands of dead young men."[2] As the cataclysm drew near, something was ending, and disappearing forever.

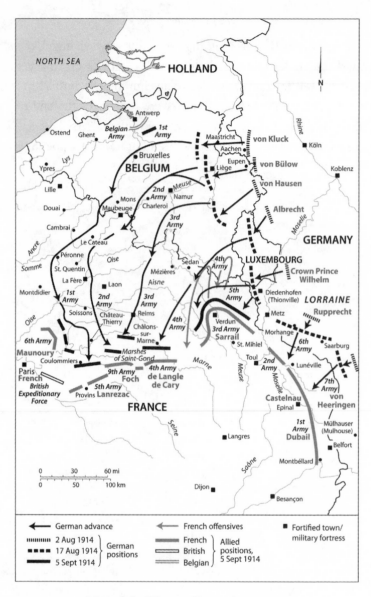

Map of the Western Front, August 1914

August 1914

CHAPTER ONE

War Breaks Out

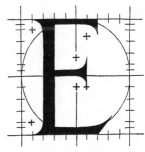VERYTHING happened quite quickly. At first, a simple, metallic tolling resounded in the distance. Then the sound grew more urgent, like a racing heartbeat, and soon the bells' solemn roar spread and filled the air. Some witnesses later recalled the suffocating heat and the dusty white roads of a landscape where everything seemed to point toward the coming storm. It was harvest time. An old world, centered on routines that had existed since time immemorial, was on the brink of the unknown.

In those days, everybody knew instinctively that the tocsin announced some kind of catastrophe, usually a fire. But at the end of this particular afternoon, most people sensed that something else was going on: the general mobilization. The threat of war had been on everyone's lips for several days. It was vaguely accepted, but no one knew exactly what it meant. A simple show of strength to intimidate Germany? A short-term combat? An elderly woman from Saint-Lormel in Brittany seemed to know: "Here it is; the bell is tolling for our boys," she murmured. Interrupted in the middle of their harvest work, the men rushed back to the village.

In the cities, the news spread by rumor. In every village, the mayor or his deputy had received the mobilization order by phone between four and five o'clock in the afternoon. The prefecture had relayed the order on behalf of the Ministry of War. They had spent the day waiting for the fateful call. As the deputy mayor of Montjoux (near Montélimar, in southeastern France) remembered it, "By eight o'clock in the morning, we had been asked not to leave the office, in view of the serious prospects ahead. Every time the phone rang, we felt agitated. We stayed close to the phone at all times." Then came the gendarmes, on horseback or by car. They brought with them the official announcement, enclosed in a black-bordered envelope, as if it were a mourning card: "The general mobilization has been announced. The first day to report is Sunday, August 2." The mayor ordered the *garde champêtre*, the village guard, to pass the word, and so messengers set out at once to carry the news to the neighboring hamlets. They had to act quickly, since the first men due to report had to leave in several hours.

Posters were put up on the wall of every town hall, school, and post office; groups formed around them. In Petits-Robins-de-Livron, some seventy-five miles south of Lyon, a veteran of the Franco-Prussian War warned, "It will be hard! I know them. There are a lot of them. We've got to be especially wary of the traps they'll set for us." Indeed, memories of

1870 were what immediately came to mind. Sometimes, as in the village of Rémuzat (about sixty miles northeast of Avignon), the mayor made an impromptu speech reminding everyone of their duty and calling on men to take a close look at their military papers.[1] There they would find the procedures to follow, the calendar showing when they would be marching with their units again, and details on what to bring with them: two shirts, a pair of underwear, two handkerchiefs, a good pair of shoes, and a day's worth of food. The authorities also sought to reassure wives and mothers. In the absence of those called up, the men who remained behind—old men, or those still waiting to be mobilized—would organize things to help bring in the harvest. "This doesn't mean war," some said. But no one quite wanted to believe these comforting words.

"they've assassinated jaurès!"

By the morning of August 1, most newspapers had already limited themselves to printing in a simple one-sheet format, with news on the front and the back. Editors realized that paper would be rationed and that some staff would be mobilized. Antoine Delécraz, an occasional contributor to the weekly *L'Illustration*, wrote in his notebook, "It smells like war."[2] Several hours before the official announcement, how many people saw the war as inescapable? How many believed that there was one last chance for peace? In the last days of July, city dwellers gradually became aware of the gravity of the situation through reading the newspapers. But not everyone believed that war was therefore inevitable. Rural France, for its part, was not as well informed, especially concerning the main event of the past twenty-four hours: the assassination, the previous evening, of Jean Jaurès. Only left-wing activists and newspaper readers drew a connection between the murder of the fifty-four-year-old Socialist leader, an ardent defender of peace, and the threat of a European war.

The Socialist politician René Viviani, who was both minister of foreign affairs and président du Conseil, paid homage to Jaurès's memory with a solemn proclamation published in the newspapers.[3] Viviani also appealed to the patriotism of the working class: "In these difficult days and in the interest of peace, [Jaurès] used his authority to support the government's patriotic action." It was necessary for the population as a whole to continue on this path and renounce "increasing public emotion via any disturbances that would throw the capital into disorder." Albert Thomas, a deputy for the Seine department and a major figure of French socialism, published an editorial in the Socialist newspaper *L'Humanité*: "Comrades of the party, union members, . . . we understand your pain, your rage. We say to you: 'Keep your sang-froid. Be calm! Be, as he would wish, worthy of your organization . . . and of the great cause he served! Be faithful to his method!'" Thomas exhorted workers, thus opening the door to the national unity government known as the Union sacrée.[4]

In reality the French government was relieved, and doubtless a bit surprised, by the moderate reaction of labor union members and members of the French Section of the Workers' International (SFIO). When the news of Jaurès's death reached them on July 31, shortly after 10 o'clock at night, the Council of Ministers had been at the Élysée Palace, the official residence and office of the president of the Republic, since the beginning of the evening. It was their third meeting of the day. Adolphe Messimy, the minister of war, had just given a presentation on immediate measures to take in the event of war, and the Council had unanimously decided to hold off on arresting suspicious foreigners, anarchists, syndicalists, and left-wing activists. Such arrests had been planned for in a government file called the Carnet B, containing the names of persons thought likely to disrupt a general mobilization. The file was established in 1886 and updated in 1909 in order to forestall trouble if war were imminent.[5] At that very moment, a doorkeeper gave Messimy a note from his orderly: one of the minister's friends wanted urgently to speak to him.

Captain Georges Ladoux of French military intelligence was admitted to the Council's meeting, followed by Célestin Hennion, préfet de police de Paris. They brought the news of Jaurès's assassination. Hennion was quite alarmed. He said that revolution would break out in three hours. As a precautionary measure, the mounted cavalry regiments that had been scheduled to leave for the German border were kept in Paris. Several ministers congratulated themselves for not implementing the measures set forth in the Carnet B; in the circumstances, it would have been a foolish provocation. Telegrams sent by préfets to the minister of the interior confirm this judgment. "By hasty incarcerations, we would risk compromising patriotic feeling in several working-class areas," wrote the préfet of the department of the Nord. According to the préfet of the Haute-Garonne, "It is of great interest to avoid the conflicts that would result from applying all the Carnet B's measures."[6]

Spontaneous demonstrations broke out near the offices of *L'Humanité* (located in the 2nd arrondissement) and were closely monitored. Around midnight, the demonstrators, at first in a state of shock, began to show signs of anger. Workers walked from the suburbs to file down the Grands Boulevards, singing the "Internationale." In his diary, the historian and monarchist journalist Jacques Bainville wrote, "One had the illusion at that moment that a revolutionary movement was beginning." However, the immense crowd that had slowly gathered following the announcement of Jaurès's death had nothing revolutionary about it. Their faces were serious and reflective. Near the place Gambetta, the police had charged at demonstrators and carried out arrests. The rumor spread that an activist had been killed in Belleville, a working-class area. After things calmed down, the groups of grieving Socialists dispersed.

At dawn, the minister of the interior had to recognize that he had been alarmed for no reason. Left-wing newspapers, printed with a black border, followed the leaders of the SFIO in calling for a dignified response to Jaurès's death. "The assassin has been arrested, he will be punished," Viviani promised. No one alluded to the many who had formerly called for the murder of the "traitor Jaurès," the "agent of the German party," and who could legitimately be held responsible for his death. Consider, for example, the nationalist politician Maurice Barrès. In 1913, during the debates over the Three-Years Law (which proposed extending military service from two to three years), Jaurès had opposed the extension, calling instead for a reorganization of the French army's reserves. Barrès accused him of acting in Germany's interests:

"[Jaurès] has half left France. . . . His thoughts are now already more German than French. . . . He can be a deputy in the Reichstag as well as in the Palais Bourbon." The monarchist writer Léon Daudet, for his part, said, "Jaurès must be seen not only as a disastrous example of a parliamentary agitator, but also as the intermediary between German corruption and the corrupt French anti-militarists. . . . A serious inquiry carried out by a national authority would reveal, in the full extent of his articles and speeches, the stains of German money. . . . It would be good to keep an eye on this traitor."[7]

On the morning of August 1, the Socialist newspaper *La Guerre sociale* limited itself to the headline "National Defense First! They've Assassinated Jaurès! We Won't Assassinate France!" The newspaper was run by Gustave Hervé, known for his antimilitarism. In Paris, the director of the municipal police offered a reassuring midmorning report: "The workers, the shopkeepers, and the middle class were painfully surprised but were talking much more about the current state of Europe. They seem to see Jaurès's death as being linked to much more dramatic current events." Moreover, the préfets' reports made no mention of any outbursts at the announcement of the assassination. Jaurès had been a deputy for the Tarn department in southwest France; the people of Carmaux were in mourning for the man they had elected to the Chamber of Deputies. In the town of Albi, the prefecture of the Tarn, a poster calling for a meeting to organize a protest was covered over (at the préfet's order) with a poster containing Viviani's appeal for national unity. In working-class cities such as Montceau-les-Mines in Burgundy, demonstrations amounted to nothing more than a rally at the labor union headquarters, where speakers lauded "the unity of all Frenchmen in the face of common dangers."[8]

In northern France, one official's report concluded that in Valenciennes, "the death of Citizen Jaurès, Deputy for the Tarn, although a cause of sadness to the Socialists and labor union members of the district, did not provoke and doubtless will not provoke any trouble." Emotions ran high, however, throughout northern France: in Denain, French flags had been tied up with black bands. In areas with less of a left-wing tradition, a kind of indifference prevailed, or worries about international events rather than national politics. In any event, in view of the danger threatening the country, discordant voices tended to give way in favor of the message of national union.

The information concerning the identity of the murderer, which began to circulate as early as the morning of August 1, contributed to strengthening this initial impulse to support the union sacrée.[9] Newspapers gave a detailed account of the assassination. After spending the day in the Chamber of Deputies and at the Ministry of Foreign Affairs, in order to question the young undersecretary Abel Ferry on the last possible chances for peace, Jean Jaurès had gone to the offices of *L'Humanité* at the end of the afternoon. He had to prepare his editorial for the following day. About 9:00, he left to go to dinner at Le Croissant, rue Montmartre, not too far from the newspaper offices. Waiting for him there were Georges Weil, SPD deputy for Alsace-Lorraine in the Reichstag, Jean Longuet and Pierre Renaudel of the SFIO, and about ten other people. "It's going badly," Jaurès told his friends, explaining what he had done that afternoon. Ernest Poisson, an editor at *L'Humanité*, arrived a little late, accompanied by his wife: "It was hot, the windows were open. . . . Behind the fashionable lace curtain in the window, there was Jaurès! However, they didn't usually sit at that table. He had his back to me. With my hand outstretched, I could touch his hair, for on his side, on my left, the curtain was pushed back a bit and in the opening between its fold and the wall, just his head could be seen." Around 9:40, as Jaurès was getting ready to get up from the table, the curtain behind him was lifted slightly and a young man fired at close range. Jaurès fell over on Renaudel. There was shouting: "They've killed Jaurès! They've killed Jaurès!"

The assassin did not try to flee. He was arrested at once and led to the police station in the rue du Mail. He did not contest the facts but at first refused to give his name, because he wanted to be the one to inform his family of his arrest. Raoul Villain, twenty-eight, was the son of a clerk in the Reims tribunal. He had studied archaeology at the École du Louvre, and he was renting a room at 44, rue d'Assas. He had no regrets: "If I committed this act, it was because Monsieur Jaurès has betrayed his country in leading a campaign against the Three-Years Law. I think that traitors should be punished and that one can give one's life for such a cause." He claimed no particular political affiliation. Maurice Pujo, one of the founders of the extreme right-wing Action Française movement, seized on this right away, and not without some relief. His organization correctly "refused to believe the perpetrator was a *Camelot du Roi* [a member of Action Française's youth section] in spite of rumors to that effect." He added that the assassination of Jaurès was "a serious error against France" in the circumstances.

Rumors, as is often the case, sought to give a semblance of meaning to an incomprehensible event: some saw the hand of "German agents provocateurs" at work,[10] others "the hand of nationalism"; still others, later on, subscribed to the idea of a Russian plot, or one by the Jesuits.[11] Fearing reprisals from left-wing activists, Pujo personally telephoned the offices of *L'Humanité* to condemn the assassination. Daudet decided that it would be prudent to leave Paris for several days. It was during the course of his night journey to Touraine that he suffered the serious automobile accident that nearly cost him his life. On the morning of August 1, Maurice Barrès had a letter delivered to Jaurès's twenty-three-year-old daughter Madeleine: "I loved your father even when our ideas put us at odds, when I had to resist the affinity that drew me to him. This assassination, at a moment when the unity of all Frenchmen has been accomplished, is a cause for national mourning." In private, the writer Charles Péguy, who had called for Jaurès to be shot by firing squad as soon as war was declared, admitted, "I am indeed obliged to say to all the Socialists whom I meet that this is abominable. And yet, this man had such a capacity for capitulation. . . . What would he have done in the case of a defeat?"[12]

Once it was clear that Raoul Villain was not a militant nationalist but a psychologically troubled young man, "a loner who was only following the instinct of a diseased brain" (*La Petite République*), it was necessary to see that Jaurès's funeral, scheduled for August 4, did not lead to outbursts. The government discreetly made contact with the SFIO, Marcel Sembat and Pierre Renaudel in particular, during the night of July 31–August 1, to ask them to calm public opinion. A meeting of the Socialist parliamentary group, and then of several of Jaurès's closest friends, took place in the early afternoon of August 1. Jaurès's wife, Louise, who had been on vacation at their house in southwest France, was due back. In reality, the emotions raised by the Socialist leader's death would soon be overshadowed by a much larger event: the announcement of the general mobilization.

FROM PEACE TO WAR

At what moment did that day of August 1 irrevocably lead to war? By the 1920s, many French and German historians were asking this question.[13] Those academic historians who had survived the Great War had formerly maintained close professional, intellectual, and friendly ties; the conflict subsequently distanced them from each other, to the point of tenacious hatred. After the war they would slowly have to learn to speak and work together again. To write the history of August 1—that is to say, the history of the irreversible passage from peace to war—meant establishing responsibility for the start of the conflict. Document versus document, diplomatic dispatch versus diplomatic dispatch; with their own weapons, academic debates continued the political confrontations of the First World War, and in a way, the war itself.

With time, our understanding of the last hours of the prewar period has evolved, and today we can better see the cultural background, the fears and anxieties that carried decisive weight in the choice to go to war.[14] For example, in their August 3 editions, the national newspapers described at length the drama playing out in Paris, with the repeated visits of the German ambassador to the Ministry of Foreign Affairs. The president of the Republic and the président du Conseil, Raymond Poincaré and René Viviani, differed in their viewpoints. And so, debates continued at the heart of the government and in the Chamber of Deputies. This complex network of diplomatic rituals and political decisions linked to national interests and personal rivalries echoed other diplomatic crises at work all across Europe: the general mobilization in Russia, the mobilization of Austria-Hungary declaring war on Serbia, the *Kriegsgefahrzustand*, or threatening danger of war, declared by Germany, and the ultimatum sent to St. Petersburg.

Nevertheless, it is worth telling the story of the diplomatic crisis of August 1 within the French context. It allows us to take into account the unknowns, the uncertainties, and the ambiguities surrounding the decisions made by French leaders, and to explain why these decisions were not always made at an opportune time. To take one example, on the evening of July 31, the German ambassador Baron Wilhelm von Schoen went first to Matignon (the official residence and office of the président du Conseil) in order to warn Viviani of the steps undertaken concerning Russia: several hours earlier, Germany had demanded that Russia stop its mobilization and specified a time frame for the Russian response to this demand. What were the intentions of the French government and how much time had it allowed to decide whether to support its Russian ally in the crisis? This was what von Schoen wanted to know.

France was in fact somewhat ill-informed at this hour regarding Russia's mobilization and plans with regard to Austria-Hungary and Germany. Although Russia had begun to mobilize on July 30, Maurice Paléologue, the French ambassador to Russia, did not warn his government until mid-morning of July 31, with a dispatch sent via Bergen in Norway. The contents of the dispatch did not reach Viviani until that evening. At the same moment, the Council of Ministers was holding an urgent meeting, where they were especially preoccupied by the news of Jaurès's assassination and by the political consequences that might arise from his death. Why had Paléologue taken more than twenty-four hours to notify Paris? Historians have long emphasized the French ambassador's responsibility in aggravating the diplomatic crisis—without, however, explaining the reasons for this unusual delay. We now tend to think that Russian leaders were keeping him out of the loop.

In any case, during the meeting with Baron von Schoen on the evening of July 31, the French were only partially informed of the situation in Russia. Moreover, when they did learn of the Russian mobilization, they wanted to believe that it was in response to the general mobilization decreed previously by Austria-Hungary, although chronology indicates exactly the opposite. It was indeed St. Petersburg that mobilized first, followed by Vienna and then Berlin. Several months later, when Viviani chose to publish the diplomatic dispatches of summer 1914 in order to justify himself, his account of the successive mobilizations relied on this official version: "Because of Austria's general mobilization and the mobilization measures that Germany has secretly but continuously undertaken for six days, the order of general mobilization has been issued to the Russian army, since Russia cannot, without the greatest danger, be caught unprepared. . . . For pressing strategic reasons, the Russian government, knowing that Germany was arming, could no longer delay converting its partial mobilization into a general one." It is easy to imagine that von Schoen and Viviani were talking past each other when they met on the evening of July 31. The former referred to war only as a danger—the meaning of the state of *Kriegsgefahrzustand* that Germany had just declared—and not as a given or as an intention on the part of his country; the latter, not having yet received official notification of the Russian mobilization, asked for time to reflect.

The ambassador then got up from his armchair and declared to the président du Conseil, "If I am forced to leave Paris, I count on you to be so good as to facilitate my departure." Then, moving to get his hat, von Schoen requested that Viviani provide him the necessary papers to leave the French capital as quickly as possible. Stunned, the head of the government reminded him that the Austrian ambassador was still in Paris and that this decision to leave hastily, without orders, could have grave consequences. Pierre de Margerie, the director of political affairs at the Ministry of Foreign Affairs, turned toward von Schoen at that moment: "You have given proof of moderation throughout your entire career—you cannot end your career with bloodshed." Von Schoen said nothing at first, but then he agreed to come back for a reply to the question of French support to Russia. A new meeting was scheduled for the next day.

Early in the morning of Saturday, August 1, a specially convened meeting of the Council of Ministers was held at the Élysée. At 11 o'clock, Viviani had to leave in order to meet with Baron von Schoen, who was waiting for him at the

Ministry of Foreign Affairs. Clearly, the German ambassador had decided, this time, to act as if he sought appeasement. He assured the président du Conseil of his attachment to France and that all his efforts would go toward preserving peace. There was no longer any question of the time frame for a final date or of obtaining papers to leave. Von Schoen sought above all to justify his country's position in reminding Viviani that it was Russia who had accelerated the crisis by mobilizing.

Was it still possible to lean on St. Petersburg and to avoid war? Moreover, was Berlin resolved to go to war? The historian Pierre Renouvin has shed some important light on these questions.[15] As he explains, in the unlikely event that France would have chosen to remain neutral, the German government had decided to ask for the return of the fortresses of Toul and Verdun as a guarantee: an unacceptable demand in the eyes of the French, and one that would have made war inevitable.[16] The text of Germany's ultimatum to Belgium was ready, and it had been sent to the German representative in Belgium by July 29. Finally, as soon as Germany had proclaimed the *Kriegsgefahrzustand* on July 31, it had been decided that the order to mobilize would be issued at the end of the afternoon of August 1, around 5 PM.

However, at the Élysée, Viviani seemed almost relaxed. Here is the account of President Poincaré: "[Viviani] announced to the assembled ministers that the ambassador had spoken no more of his departure and that everything was perhaps about to be settled. I would like to hope so, but I have the feeling that Monsieur de Schoen did not come yesterday evening and this morning in order to settle for a dilatory reply." Published in the second half of the 1920s, Poincaré's memoirs seek to portray him as a peaceful and determined man, careful to make use of all means possible to avoid war. Doubtless he wanted first of all to justify himself and respond to the attacks naming him one of the principal figures responsible for the conflict. He was accused of giving carte blanche to the Russians during his trip to St. Petersburg at the end of July, getting caught up in the hellish spiral of alliances. Such accusations—"Poincaré's war," as it was said at the time—were still numerous in the immediate postwar period. If we limit ourselves to the version provided by his memoirs, it seems clear that the German leaders are notably duplicitous, while the two heads of the French government seem to have done everything to preserve peace.

As it happens, August 1 as retrospectively described in the memoirs does not correspond to the daily notes Poincaré made in his diary. According to the memoirs, the president of the Republic and the président du Conseil agreed to treat the crisis with tact, and the one who sometimes lost his sang-froid was Viviani rather than Poincaré. Nothing of the sort appears in the daily notes. Thus, on July 31, when the German ambassador came to inform Viviani of the Russian mobilization and to ask him what France planned to do, Viviani put off the question by arguing that peace was not yet compromised: "Let me still hope that extreme decisions can be avoided." If Poincaré's journal can be believed, however, it was he who asked Viviani to be much more firm and to answer that France would act according to its interests. At the end of the morning of August 1, according to the memoirs, Poincaré greeted with irony Viviani's triumphal return from his meeting with the

German ambassador. In his diary, he shows himself to be much more biting: "Not so much optimism, I beg of you. . . . It is clear that [von Schoen] wants to remain several more days in Paris in order to amuse us." Poincaré's portrait of the président du Conseil, in this document written day by day, is unsparing: "Viviani, who lets himself be affected by contradictory impressions with disconcerting ease, is very somber at times and then tries to come up with a miracle that could still fix everything." On July 27, while both men were on the way back from their trip to Russia, Poincaré had already noted, "[Viviani] is nervous, agitated, and makes imprudent pronouncements and judgments that show a complete ignorance of foreign affairs."[17]

Two radically different visions, then, of these decisive hours in the diplomatic crisis, and two portraits of the French head of state, levelheaded in one case, in the other willingly bellicose toward Germany, critical of Viviani, and even manipulative. Particularly revealing is the role that military authorities play in Poincaré's memoirs and in his daily notes. At midafternoon on July 31, General Joseph Joffre, chief of the General Staff since 1911, had sent Adolphe Messimy, the minister of war, an alarming note concerning troop movements already under way in Germany. It concluded thus: "If the state of tension continues and if the Germans, under cover of diplomatic conversations, continue to apply their mobilization plan—which they execute all while not naming it as such—it is absolutely necessary for the government to know that starting this evening (July 31), any delay of twenty-four hours in calling up the reservists and in sending the telegram for the covering force[18] will mean a retreat of our concentration plan, that is to say, initially abandoning part of our territory, some ten to twelve miles per day of delay."[19]

The following days, the confirmation of the Russian mobilization (July 30) and the Austro-Hungarian (July 31), as well as new German reinforcements on the border with France, necessitated immediate action. In his memoirs, Poincaré recounts that Joffre went to the Ministry of War to meet Messimy at 8 AM on August 1: "If the government delays in issuing the order for a general mobilization, it will be impossible for me to continue to take on the heavy responsibility of [my] high-level duties," he explained to the minister of war, who hurried to the Élysée, accompanied by the chief of the General Staff. Poincaré allegedly agreed to Joffre himself presenting his case to the Council of Ministers, which was meeting that morning. Describing this day later, the last day before the storm, Poincaré stressed the army's influence on the executive branch. He depicts Joffre as a "calm and decided man" who managed to obtain the proclamation of a general mobilization thanks to his information regarding the mobilization in Germany, and thanks to a logic that was difficult to contradict: in a situation as complex as the start of a war, where each hour counts, France risked finding itself "in an irremediable state of inferiority" if it allowed the German mobilization to get an edge.

The latest news from Germany was, it was true, rather troubling. The Schlieffen Plan, named after the former chief of the German General Staff, had since 1905 spelled out the organization of German mobilization and the first weeks of the war. This plan relied on a key factor: swiftness of movement. French troops would find themselves enveloped by a vast movement of German troops turning across Belgium and the north of France, and would be conquered in a few weeks. The Germans, assured of their success, had struck a commemorative medal for the capture of Paris; it featured the Arc de Triomphe and a dual inscription above it: 1871 and 1914.[20] Taking into account the slow Russian mobilization, Germany would have all the time it needed to win on the Western Front before returning to the Eastern Front. The entire war in the west was supposed to last only six weeks. Requisitions and the purchase of horses had begun on July 30, perhaps earlier, for everything had to be ready to transport troops and matériel to the French and Belgian borders as soon as the mobilization was announced. Five contingents of reservists had been called back, and covering units had been established along the entire border. Joffre remarked, "It can, therefore, be said that on August 4th, even without the order for mobilization having been issued, the German Army will be entirely mobilized; in this way a start of over forty-eight hours, perhaps of three days, will have been secured."[21]

If Poincaré's memoirs are to be believed, it was thus the chief of the General Staff who persuaded the executive branch to take action. However, in his own memoirs of this period, Joffre does not mention being present himself at the Council of Ministers during the morning of August 1. The decision to mobilize did indeed come from the president of the Republic and without any pressure, it seems, from the army. Here is what Poincaré wrote in his notes on the evening of August 1: "Yesterday, we had decided in principle that the order to mobilize would go out today. It had to be issued before six o'clock in the evening. Messimy had had everything ready since yesterday, but when Viviani arrived at the Council, beaming, I saw the moment when, after Schoen's visit as described by Viviani, yesterday's decision was going to have to be given up. But this morning I saw General Joffre in Messimy's presence, and he told me there would be serious problems if we postponed it. I indicated strongly to the Council that I would not go back on the decision taken in principle yesterday evening. Everyone ended by approving of what I said."[22] Yet another difference between his daily notes and his memoirs, according to whether Poincaré describes his daily work as chief of state or whether, some ten years later, he seeks to clear himself of having wanted and caused the war.

Whatever the case may be, the mobilization order, signed by Poincaré, Viviani, Minister of the Navy Armand Gauthier, and Messimy, was indeed handed over to the minister of war at the end of the Council of Ministers' meeting, with the proviso to hold off until the middle of the afternoon, that is, until the last possible moment to start the mobilization on August 2. No one knows quite why the text, signed around noon, was kept secret for nearly four hours. "At 1530 hours, the fatal hour having arrived, I sent General Ebener to get [the mobilization order]," wrote Joffre. "At 1555 hours, the prepared telegrams were taken to the post and telegraph office in the rue de Grenelle and immediately sent out all over France."

To prevent Germany from invoking French aggression as a cause for war, which would have freed Great Britain from the defensive agreement signed with France, the Council of Ministers decided on July 30 to pull the troops six miles back from the border. Military leaders did not take this news well, for they viewed it as a symbolic sign of weakness in response to the enemy. "For national reasons of a moral nature and for pressing reasons of a diplomatic nature, it is indispensable to leave to the Germans all responsibility for inciting hostilities," Joffre noted, however, in his instructions to his commanders. "Until further notice, the frontier covering force will be limited to pushing any attacking troops back over the border, without further pursuit and without entering enemy territory." Whoever might cross this six-mile line would be subject to court-martial. At the same time, France reaffirmed its respect for Belgium's and Luxembourg's neutrality. In case of German invasion of either of these countries, France nonetheless reserved the right to enter their territory in its turn, in order to defend itself.

"A FEW WORDS, SO SIMPLE AND SO TERRIBLE"

In the abundance of firsthand accounts of August 1, 1914—daily notes, correspondence, memoirs written during the war or in the 1920s—people describe at length the moment when the poster announcing the mobilization was put up. Reading this poster, the French for the first time witnessed the war's arrival as an accomplished fact, not as a more or less distant risk. It was also doubtless at this exact moment that the fears that had been growing over the past several weeks were realized. Retrospectively, the atmosphere of this early part of the month of August seemed stifling, the summer, overwhelming, the heat, unusual. "The weather is horribly stuffy," wrote Delécraz, "the air seems dense, a huge storm threatens, putting our nerves to a formidable test."[23] The war had to break out, other witnesses noted, so that all the tension could dissolve. There were many who saw signs in the preceding days, like this Parisian housewife whom a journalist overheard chatting with a neighbor: "I said so, I did, business wasn't going right anymore, things couldn't go on like this."[24]

The responses to the poster's appearance reveal how stunned people were, despite knowing that war could break out. During this feverish, rumor-filled period, the poster announcing the mobilization made this historic event suddenly appear real. "As I was going home, around 6 PM, I saw the order for mobilization in a post office," noted Baronne Michaux. "No matter how prepared I was for this outcome, when I knew it was inevitable, a violent anxiety seized me, an emotion unlike anything else in my life; I could barely get home; I was worn out."[25] Another Parisian woman testified: "What movement in Paris! My heart beating, I approached the poster. Near me, a woman almost fainted. Then there were young men who burst into a war song . . . already!"[26] Some described the poster as a piece of yellow paper, where a hasty, handwritten text announced the mobilization: this was a temporary poster, put up around midafternoon, in some Paris post offices and in the Préfecture de Police. The official poster was white, with two French flags on top, and carefully lettered; it was distributed by the gendarmerie in all the city and town halls in France around 5 PM, and the date of the first day of mobilization had been added by hand.

Initially, however, the poster escaped notice. Its presence could be remarked upon only by unusual murmurs as a group of onlookers clustered about. In Lyon, a crowd of several hundred people gathered in front of the iron gates of the city hall. In Marseille, people streamed to the Palais de la Bourse, where the poster had been put up. Antoine Delécraz, an attentive observer of Paris at this time, reported, "I followed avenue Trudaine to the place d'Anvers. In this normally peaceful neighborhood, I noted an unusual agitation. People seemed anxious. There was a group gathering at the post office. Only men: they were jostling each other in front of a small square of white paper, eight inches high and ten inches across, on which I read this laconic and terrifying handwritten text: 'Extreme urgency—official leaflet. GENERAL MOBILIZATION. First day of mobilization— Sunday, August 2.' The poster was put up at 4:45 PM. '—There it is!' This is what everyone said."[27]

The historian Daniel Halévy left the thermal springs of La Bourboule (in the Auvergne) by funicular on the morning of August 1 to go hiking in the mountains. He descended to the valley around 6 PM and came across a group of young men, who called out to him, as he describes it: "'We're mobilizing! . . . A phone call has announced it.' I felt a shock, but a light one. For me, the thing was done, psychologically, it was done. We met the drummers of the village guard. The two men stopped in front of the school, the drums rolled, and the guard read the announcement. Seven or eight people were there. We took off our hats; 'Vive la France!' cried a healthy-looking laborer. We drifted away. It seemed like we had just witnessed a scene from a play."[28] Many other witnesses described this feeling of unreality when the war was announced. The solemnity of the moment stifled all spontaneity, to the point where gestures, speeches, even feelings seemed artificial. Moreover, the event had so often been imagined and anticipated that it was almost anticlimactic when it finally happened. A small white poster on a wall; so this was the start of a war? Soldiers would write the same thing in their letters and notebooks on November 11, 1918: was this it then, the moment so long awaited?

Jacques Bainville was struck by the disproportion between the dramatic aspect of the mobilization and the apparent insignificance of the poster: "I shall always see this official white paper that, around four o'clock, appeared at the post office nearest to my house and that, at the same time, was making its journey all over France via telegraph. . . . This official telegram stayed up for a long time on the walls of city halls and train stations. Those who lived through those days have never been able to remember it without thinking: 'Here are a few words, so simple and so terrible, that decided the fate of thousands and thousands of men, the card on which a nation's destiny was played out.'"[29] In his account of Paris during the summer of 1914, another observer, Arthur-Lévy, expressed a similar sentiment: the most important event in the existence of a people took the form of a simple telegram "bearing words hastily written by hand."[30]

There was also a disproportion between the announcement of the mobilization and the reactions of people grouped in front of the posters. No shouts, no displays of collective emotion: "The crowd reads, keeps silent; some weep and some go off in silence."[31] At this very moment when everything shifted toward war, people turned to their loved ones, to the near future. Everyone doubtless imagined what the mobilization would bring with it: families separated, additional financial worries, the risk of death. In Paris, there was an agitation without disorder, without shouting; a silent agitation, so to speak. War had already irresistibly infiltrated into peacetime by means of new tension, greater seriousness, the sharp sense of individual and collective destinies. In the streets, conversations could be heard at a low, deep murmur.

Pedestrians, more numerous than usual, overflowed the sidewalks and streets. Trams had stopped running, buses had been requisitioned; people hurried home on foot, to prepare for the first wave of mobilized men to leave. The gravity of the event made people speak more openly. Strangers spoke to each other: "What day are you leaving?" and wished each other good luck. But these words were spoken in a low voice, almost whispered. And then each person went on his way, hurrying home. This quieting of city noises was the sign of a larger reorganization. "By the simple effect of thirty hastily scribbled words," Arthur-Lévy observed, "tomorrow, for the first time since France has been France, we will see all the arteries of social life brusquely cut. Tomorrow, every family will be broken up. Tomorrow, all projects, studies, and works in all branches of intellectual, commercial, and financial activity will be suspended for an unlimited amount of time."[32] Silence, made up by turns of stupor and anxiety in the face of an uncommon event, accompanied the inevitable march into the unknown.

A LAST NIGHT OF PEACE

Who can say what this last night of peace looked like, on a night when war was on everyone's minds? For some, time seemed to have sped up; for many others, it was suspended, in a sort of unreality. Antoine Delécraz decided to walk over to the Grands Boulevards. When he arrived at the Grand Café, located near the Opera, the noise of conversations, normally drowned out by traffic, caught his attention: since 6 PM, all buses had been sent back to their depots in order to be made available to military authorities. Waves of cars, normally so dense at the start of the evening, seemed mysteriously absent. Sidewalk cafés were full of people: men ready to leave the next day or in several days, foreign tourists stuck in Paris and still uncertain how to return home, and those who did not want to miss what was happening. The clientele inside the café, destined for different fates now that war had been declared, was huddled under the gleam of gilding, of mirrors, of crimson decor. People were exchanging the latest news on the mobilization, on the German threat at the borders, and on the burial of Jaurès, scheduled for Tuesday, August 4. Sometimes, groups of demonstrators passed by on the boulevard, waving the flag or singing the "Marseillaise." Mixed in with these young men were foreign volunteers, often Italians, who shouted "Vive la France!" They were greeted with a wave of the hand or a nod of the head, but Delécraz was also irritated by their boisterous attitude, which contrasted strangely with the dignified aspect of the crowd surrounding them.[33] It was the same scene in the cafés of the Latin Quarter: young men and women wore rosettes and sang patriotic songs. Couples could be seen walking by, their arms laden with packages: shops had closed late in order to allow the mobilized soldiers to buy a pair of shoes, some socks, sweaters, or belts. And soon the sky grew dark at the approach of the storm, and torrential rainfall drenched passersby, while sidewalk cafés cleared out in minutes.

At the Gare de l'Est and the Gare du Nord, onlookers watched travelers go back and forth and tried to identify the shadows slipping inside: railway personnel and reservists who had been called up, foreign families fleeing the chaos of war. A sign indicated that trains heading toward Germany were limited and that it was no longer possible to go to Alsace-Lorraine. Another sign indicated that the train heading for Cologne would henceforth go only as far as Verviers, about eighteen miles from the border between Belgium and Germany. In reality, all communication with Germany had been cut: roads, railways, telegraph, telephone . . . For security reasons, only travelers with tickets or permits were authorized to access the platforms.

Soldiers from the Territorial Army had taken position in order to ward off sabotage. Toward the end of the evening, activity slowed down, since the transport of mobilized soldiers had stopped and would not resume until morning. The men who had to leave Paris at an early hour sometimes slept on the sidewalk, like the three hundred Belgian farm laborers whom Delécraz saw while passing in front of the Gare du Nord. They had been working the harvest in France, and their own mobilization was calling them home. Slowly, night enveloped the train stations. Buildings were plunged into darkness, owing to fear of air raids.

The same early evening agitation could be felt at the Gare d'Orsay, which connected Paris to the west and southwest of France. Millions of Parisians tried to flee the capital, fearing a German invasion, while many citizens from the provinces who had been staying in Paris were now making every effort to return home. Many Spaniards were leaving for Spain. The ticket windows were overwhelmed. Because trains were sporadic, travelers had to sleep in the station. Women holding children in their arms lay down where they could in the halls of the boarding platforms. Fierce battles broke out in the effort to obtain train tickets. The sidewalks were strewn with packages ripped open, men's and women's hats, umbrellas and canes, food of all kinds, and broken windows.

For Delécraz, this petit-bourgeois panic contrasted with the determination of the rest of the Paris population. "Of all the French railway networks, the Orléans network was the most encumbered with cowards, and it is hard to know what to despise the most: their selfishness or their cowardice." The figure of the shirker, which would play such an important role in the war culture of 1914–18, was already taking shape in the early hours of the mobilization, in the indignation against those who already sought to avoid the front and their patriotic duty.[34]

August 2, 1914, fell on a Sunday. Many churches were full of people. Everyone went to mass with their families. Only the villages of northeastern France were already empty of the majority of their male population. Indeed, in the regions near the German border, troops had received the order to get under way on July 31. They were the ones charged with heading off any enemy incursion and with covering the zone called the "concentration," where the regiments would form the order of battle during the next days. "In three hours, we will head to an unknown place, we will have the honor of being the first to fight," wrote a member of the 22nd Dragoon Regiment of Reims. "It is we who will keep watch on the border while the rest of the army mobilizes."[35]

By the morning of Friday, July 31, a resident of Reims had noticed an unusual agitation in the barracks neighborhood. Dozens of horses were being led to the requisition department by their owners. Reservists were presenting themselves one by one at the door of the regiment, wearing their campaign uniform. A curious crowd had gathered to encourage them. There were women, as well as many children. A continual flood of regimental cyclists and cars was leaving in all directions. By nightfall, two regiments of cavalry had left their quarters; it was said that they were heading toward the town of Sedan in the Ardennes. During the same time, men of the Territorial Army, aged thirty-four to forty-nine years old, had received their official orders. Some were heading to guard the railways and military and public buildings. Others would take up administrative duties in places like the post office.[36]

In the villages adjoining the border, emotions ran even higher, for people feared a sudden attack by German patrols. In Réméréville (east of Nancy) during the night of July 31, a gendarme went from house to house to distribute individual call-up orders to reservists. The hurried notice of the departure cut farewells short. After the men left, women stayed behind, chatting on their doorsteps. On August 2, bells rang for mass. In the church, the right-hand side, the men's side, was almost empty. Only some old men remained, and their voices were covered over by the women's singing.[37]

The men got under way by groups, heading toward the nearest train station. Each group was off to the city housing its regiment. Their luggage was often a simple bundle carried over the shoulder or a small suitcase, which made them look like travelers. They set forth with a firm footstep and a serious look, too stern to be going to a wedding, too dressed up in their Sunday best for a country fair. At that time, France was covered by a multitude of small railway networks that have long since disappeared. Ordinarily, there were not many reasons to take the train. For trips during the workday, people preferred to go on foot or in a horse-drawn cart. There were few bicycles at the time, and even fewer cars in the countryside. Here is what we find in the mobilization instructions for a farmer from Crasville, a small village of three hundred inhabitants on the eastern side of the Manche department, in Normandy: "The soldier will travel for free by railway. He will take with him a day's worth of food, and a helmet if he has one. He will present himself, along with this document, at the train station of Anneville-Crasville before 8 o'clock in the morning on the third day of the mobilization, and he will take the train indicated to him by the stationmaster. He will get off the train at Cherbourg and will immediately go to the police station, where he will be shown the way to his unit in Cherbourg, in the Rochambeau barracks."

All across France, thousands of stationmasters had unsealed a letter sent to them on August 1, at the same time as the order to mobilize. The letter described which trains would be passing through their station, how many cars they would contain, and their specific schedules. These were various pieces of an unusual puzzle that was being assembled minute by minute. The wheels of peacetime had ceased to function. Other mechanisms were being engaged, carefully prepared by armies of engineers, geographers, and technicians. The railway service had mobilized all its available trains, including freight and cattle cars. Men piled in, the train left the station, and with it, a familiar space, its small towns and church bells passing by the train windows at a quickening pace.

In the space of a day, barracks towns and cities were overcome with conscripts. They called out to each other in the streets; they were grouped together according to their villages of origin. To ease their anxiety, they talked of harvest time, of how work in the fields was getting on and the latest news from their villages, or they boasted, mocking these Germans who dared to attack France. Emboldened by the shouts and insults thrown at an enemy still out of range, some quickly sketched on the walls: a pig's head surmounted by a spiked helmet, or a ridiculous face covered by a gigantic moustache. The most vehement promised to skin Kaiser Bill. They were really going to show him who was the strongest! How hot it was in the late afternoon, and there was no more room in the sidewalk cafés. People raised their glasses to the first soldiers to be mobilized. Had the Germans already attacked? Where would the regiment be sent? People also wondered how long the war would last; the most pessimistic put it at around Christmastime.

The men then returned to their barracks in order to prepare for departure. Because of the territorial organization of the French army in 1914, men from the same region were grouped together in the same barracks, such as residents of the pays de Léon, in the 19th Infantry from Brest, and those from Trégor in the 48th Infantry from Guingamp, for example. The French army of summer 1914 was made up of "civilians in uniform," of citizen-soldiers still deeply linked to their peacetime habits. At a fundamental level, the army was mainly made up of men from rural France. Their identity was formed by the boundaries of their land, their region, their own *petite patrie*. During their first night in the barracks, the men rediscovered the spaces, gestures, and rituals of their military service. It was not quite peacetime, and not quite war. But the bells that had tolled for the mobilization only the day before already seemed to belong to a distant world.

CHAPTER TWO

Visions of War, Dreams of Peace

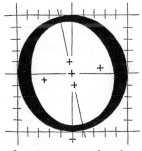N August 2, 1914, war became a re-
ality. Later, in a speech commemo-
rating the fiftieth anniversary of the
mobilization, General de Gaulle
described it as the day "when all the
French stood together in unity. . . .
Every region, locality, and category
of society, every family and every soul were suddenly in agreement. The political, social, and religious quarrels dividing the
country were erased in an instant. Certainly . . . the strict and
equal obligations of military service, combined with the call
to mobilize and rejoin military units, the requisitions, and
transports all encouraged people to support the war effort. . . .
But the country's immense energy that day was driven by a
shared certainty that France faced the greatest danger, and
had to be saved forever."[1]

Since this time, the Union sacrée has been one of the
greatest political myths of modern France. In the 1960s,

33

Gaullist rhetoric contrasted the France of 1940—divided, weakened, and conquered—with the France of 1914, united in a common cause. In both cases, the reality was obviously more complex. Contradictory attitudes in public opinion, along with regional diversity and a great variety of expressions of patriotism, all marked the early days of August 1914. To describe France in the summer of 1914 is to restore this complexity. Three days elapsed between the time when the notice of the general mobilization was posted (August 1) and the president of the Republic's call for the country to form a Union sacrée (August 4). In the course of those three days, millions of men exchanged their civilian clothes for military uniforms. Initially, on August 2, they were simply men mobilized to join their regiments; the next day, they were fighting for a country officially at war with Germany. In several days, the open opposition to the war typical of left-wing pacifism fell silent. Initial shock gave way to a firm resolve: France had been attacked and must be defended.

PROBABLE AND YET UNEXPECTED

In the early days of August 1914, the French seemed united behind their political and military leaders and soldiers. Numerous civilians came out to cheer on the troops. Flags and bunting were everywhere: in the streets, on government buildings, and hanging from balconies. Yet the images that remain of this extraordinary moment are both authentic and misleading. Photographs of the crowds of soldiers milling in train stations have given the impression that this moment was carefree, even joyous. As the French expression had it, the soldier went off to war "la fleur au fusil," with great enthusiasm—literally, with a flower in the barrel of his rifle. The reality was different, for the very simple reason that the war had taken the French by surprise. "How can we explain that the war, which had been so often foreseen and predicted since 1905, seemed to fall on the world like an avalanche when it broke out in the summer of 1914?" the historian Jules Isaac has asked.

Probable and yet unexpected: this is the first paradox of France's going to war in 1914. The risk of a conflict between European nations had been clear, but in what time frame and under what conditions? For some years, two alliances had been at odds with each other: in 1879, Germany had signed a military agreement with Austria-Hungary, which Italy would join in 1882. This triple alliance depended especially on the entente between Berlin and Vienna, for Italy had gradually become closer to France. In June 1902, a secret agreement had even been signed between Rome and Paris, according to which Italy would maintain strict neutrality in case of war between France and Germany. For their part, France and the United Kingdom had signed the Entente cordiale in 1904, after having been on the brink of war six years earlier during the Fashoda incident of 1898. This entente would grow to include Russia, a French ally since 1893. But the Triple Entente was as unstable as the Triple Alliance. Politically, the authoritarian czarist regime and Republican France did not have much in common. Moreover, Russia's influence in Europe had been considerably weakened by its defeat in the Russo-Japanese War of 1904–5.

It is necessary, however, not to ascribe too much importance to this diplomatic arrangement; it did not automatically lead to the start of hostilities, as has sometimes been thought. In a conflict like the First World War, circumstance, perceptions of enemy forces, the passions of public opinion, and a kind of collective blindness played just as great a role as did military alliances conceived years before and in another context.[2]

At the dawn of the twentieth century, Europeans often saw war as probable, even inevitable. For example, an editorial writer for the *Nouvelle Revue* wrote on January 1, 1912, "We will have war. . . . After forty years of peace armed to the teeth, we can finally write this sentence without making readers of a French journal tremble in terror or leap indignantly from their chairs."[3] A year later, the historian Pierre Albin, author of *L'Allemagne et la France en Europe (1885–1894)*, took a more measured tone: "That day when the conflict will break out is perhaps a distant one. It may never come. The governments in power at that moment will perhaps hesitate when faced with the horrifying responsibility of this war, next to which the wars of the past will seem like children's games. But the risk of war exists, no impartial man can deny it."[4]

When exactly did this growing awareness of the risk of war begin? No one can say with certainty. Was it during the first Moroccan Crisis (March–April 1905)? This occurred when Kaiser Wilhelm II spoke out against the French protectorate of Morocco while on an official visit to that country. At the time, the diplomatic crisis made a strong impression. The président du Conseil, Maurice Rouvier, accepted the resignation of Minister of Foreign Affairs Théophile Delcassé, who supported taking a hard line against Germany. And here is what Charles Péguy wrote in the journal *Cahiers de la*

Quinzaine: "I knew that in the space of these two hours a new period had begun in the history of my own life, and the history of the country, and assuredly in the history of the world." These lines might suggest that war was imminent, but it would not break out until nine years later.

Other major tensions preceded World War I, such as the Agadir Crisis of summer 1911. A German gunboat, SMS *Panther*, anchored off the Moroccan coast; this was a sign of hostility toward the French protectorate. Negotiations got under way in August between the président du Conseil, Joseph Caillaux, and German emissaries—against the wishes of Minister of Foreign Affairs Justin de Selves, who opposed making any concessions to Germany. In 1927, the historian Pierre Renouvin remarked: "A war adjourned is often a war avoided."[5] How many other tensions remained at a regional level rather than degenerating into conflicts on a European scale?

The prewar period can be defined by its collective fears, which the historian Jules Isaac best summed up in 1933: "Before, we spoke of peace and war, but (at least, those of us in the generations born after 1870) we didn't know what we were talking about; peace was something we were used to, it was the air that everyone breathed without thinking about it; war was a word, a purely theoretical concept. When we suddenly realized that this concept could change into reality, we felt in our entire being a shock whose memory cannot be erased."[6] What Isaac does not say, however, is that at the turn of the century, faith in modernity, technological progress, and scientific inventions went hand in hand with fear of war; in any case, the prewar period was characterized by a general feeling rather than by specific fears.

In all of Europe it was thought that only states on the rise, according to a social Darwinist perspective, could survive the competition between the major powers.[7] This attitude explains the naval competition between London and Berlin and the growth of leagues (the pan-German league, the army league, and so on) in German society. Such an attitude also fed a strong obsession with decadence, which took different forms depending on the country: fear of delayed economic growth, arms races, anxiety over demographic decline and moral degeneracy, or in Germany, the fear of being encircled by czarist Russia on one side and France and the United Kingdom on the other. In a 1912 German best-seller, *Deutschland und der Nächste Krieg* (Germany and the next war), the Prussian general Friedrich von Bernhardi portrayed his country as a "mutilated torso," while Admiral Tirpitz explained that without a sufficiently powerful battle fleet, Germany would be like "a mollusk without its shell."[8]

Far from being peaceful, the years preceding the Great War were marked by deep worries. The term that was later coined to describe this period, the Belle Époque, was a retrospective illusion. Many at the time denounced the threats facing Western civilization: Russian apocalyptic authors such as Vladimir Soloviev; those who feared the Americanization of the world, such as the British journalist William Stead; and prophets of decline like Gustave Le Bon. Others were anxious about the way that time seemed to be speeding up. Japan's victory over Russia in the battle of Tsushima in May 1905 had Westerners fearing a shift of world power toward the Far East. The Russian writer Andrei Bely denounced "the menacing specter of the Mongol invasion from the East." Other events now forgotten, such as the violent earthquake that shook the city of Messina in December 1908, were interpreted as signs foreshadowing even greater disasters. The young German painter Max Beckmann, an eager reader of Nietzsche, was inspired by descriptions of this natural disaster when creating his painting *Scene from the Destruction of Messina* (1909).

For many, a world conflict thus appeared likely. Consider these evocative titles from popular literature: *The War of the 20th Century* (Paris, 1894), *The Coming Terror* (Sydney, 1894), *How the Germans Took London: Forewarned, Forearmed* (London, 1900), *World without End* (London, 1907), *The Infernal War* (Paris, 1908), *The End of France in 19* . . (Leipzig, 1912), *How We Will Torpedo Berlin* (Paris, 1913), *The European War* (Paris, 1914).[9] In several short years, the British novelist H. G. Wells published three "invasion novels," including *The War of the Worlds* (1898) and *The War in the Air* (1908), in which he described the destruction of New York by German flying machines. In December 1904, James Barrie's play *Peter Pan* featured Captain Hook, whom contemporaries sometimes identified with Kaiser Wilhelm II and his large moustache.

Although a general anxiety dominated popular culture at the turn of the century, there was also ardent faith in human progress. The most notable example can be found in the great world's fairs, such as the one held in Paris in 1900. This world's fair would take stock of the century, in the words of Alfred Picard, one of the high-ranking French government officials in charge. To the fifty million people who came, the fair opened the door to the promises and hopes of the twentieth century—a mix of technical audacity, imperial power, and exoticism. Progress, prosperity, and modernity were openly celebrated in the same place where prophets of doom predicted war: the national pavilions of the forty countries represented, each vying to outdo the other. A profound symbol of the ambiguity of the time was the Frenchman Félix Desruelles's statue *Armed Peace*, awarded a gold medal at the fair. The statue showed Marianne with a warlike face, her right arm on her knee, and her left arm leaning on a long glaive. The tip of the sword pointed at the ground, where there were books, symbols of culture and knowledge. A single discreet olive branch, hidden by the pommel, suggested the statue's meaning. Even in a world's fair aimed at celebrating concord and progress in humankind, France sought to remind its enemies and allies that it was ready in war as in peace.

All that was left was to hope that the coming war would seem too destructive, too costly, and too absurd for modern nations to risk. Such was the argument of the British journalist Norman Angell in his book *The Great Illusion*, published in 1910. A huge best-seller translated into numerous languages, it took up ideas already developed in the six-volume work *Is War Now Impossible?* by Jan Gotlib Bloch, a Russian businessman of Polish background. Both Bloch and Angell argued that the war would result in a pyrrhic victory for the winners, since losses would come at too high a cost for the victors as well as the vanquished. War would bring with it a general economic crisis, high inflation, and serious financial disaster, none of which anyone wanted.

Here is what Bloch said to his English translator, W. T. Stead: "At first there will be increased slaughter—increased slaughter on so terrible a scale as to render it impossible to get troops to push the battle to a decisive issue. They will try to, thinking that they are fighting under the old conditions, and they will learn such a lesson that they will abandon the attempt for ever. Then, instead of a war fought out to the bitter end in a series of decisive battles, we shall have as a substitute a long period of continually increasing strain upon the resources of the combatants. The war, instead of being a hand-to-hand contest in which the combatants measure their physical and moral superiority, will become a kind of stalemate, in which neither army being able to get at the other, both armies will be maintained in opposition to each other, threatening each other, but never being able to deliver the final and decisive attack."[10]

Bloch and Angell were convinced that the world would not be crazy enough to deliberately bring about its own ruin. A French economist summed it up as follows: "A continental conflagration, involving six, eight, ten nations, great and small, would be ruinous for all of humanity." This was only six weeks before the assassination in Sarajevo.[11]

THE SLEEPING CLOUD OF WAR

Those in economic and business circles were not the only ones preoccupied by the risks of war and their ruinous consequences. The labor movement and the Socialists also devoted a considerable part of their debates to this topic. The foundational texts of Marxism had long stressed the link between a capitalist society, imperial expansion, and the risk of war. During the First Congress of the Second International in 1889, European socialists solemnly remarked that "peace was the first and indispensable condition for any emancipation of the working class" and that it was "the madness of bourgeois pacifists to want to preserve the capitalist mode of production and suppress war, its natural consequence." Jean Jaurès affirmed: "[Capitalism] carries war within it, as the sleeping cloud carries the storm."

In any case, the question was no longer whether the capitalist model contained in itself the risk of a European war but whether the concerted efforts of European socialists could avoid such a conflict. Even if a world war could lead to the destruction of capitalist society, Socialists thought that the cost in human lives would be too heavy a price to pay. Jaurès again, in May 1905: "As for us we hate war, despite the revolutionary possibilities it contains, for it also contains reactionary possibilities, as well as the certainty of barbarism and savagery. But it is good for governments to know that from the clouds of war they have brought together, the lightning bolt of revolution can emerge and strike them."[12]

Among the different branches of European socialism, opinions diverged concerning what measures to take. At the Socialist congress in Stuttgart in August 1907, the Frenchman Gustave Hervé clashed with the German August Bebel. Hervé supported a strong antimilitarist line, which meant opposing any mobilization. It would have been impossible for Bebel to take such a line in Germany. The congress concluded with a declaration of principle on the risk of war, but did not indicate specific measures to prevent it. Three years later in September 1910, the Eighth Congress of the Second International took place in Copenhagen. The Frenchman Édouard Vaillant and the Briton James Keir Hardie proposed an amendment urging a general strike in the arms and transport industries in the event of war. A large majority rejected this amendment. Delegates preferred to push back the choice of a common strategy to the next congress, scheduled for Vienna in August 1914. Obviously, this congress never took place. The basic question was this: could European socialists agree on a common plan of action, or would questions of national interest prevail?

The Balkan Wars in 1912 and 1913 further increased worries in Socialist milieus. This time, direct allies of major European powers were at war, and they used modern weapons, such as rapid-fire artillery, whose devastating effects had already been apparent during the Russo-Japanese War of 1904–5. The Balkan Wars also resulted in the massacre of civilian populations, and the Carnegie Foundation sent a commission to investigate. After five weeks on the ground, the commission concluded: "Every clause in international law relative to war on land and to the treatment of the wounded has been violated by all the belligerents." Among the multiple eyewitness testimonies to war crimes in the Balkans, a Serbian soldier wrote, in August 1913: "We imprisoned 300 Bulgarian soldiers. We were ordered to install the machine gun in a valley. I guessed the goal of these preparations. The Bulgarian prisoners watched our work and seemed to know what awaited them. We had them stand in a line. Then our machine began to work its way across the line, from one end to the other . . ."

The French popular press was full of references to the "Balkan atrocities," with color illustrations in the supplements to *Le Petit Journal.* This was the atmosphere surrounding the Extraordinary Ninth Congress of the Socialist

International in Basel in November 1912, where Louis Aragon situated the epilogue of his famous novel *Les Cloches de Bâle* (The bells of Basel, 1934). The Socialists held their meeting in the great cathedral, after crossing the old city in a procession accompanied by thousands. On November 24, Jean Jaurès gave an impassioned speech in the cathedral: "The scales of Fate waver in the hands of governments. . . . *Vivos voco, mortuous plango, fulgura frango!*[13] *Vivos voco:* I call upon the living to defend themselves against the monster on the horizon. *Mortuos plango:* I weep for the countless dead lying in the East; their votting stench fills us with remorse. *Fulgura frango:* I will destroy the lightning of war looming in the clouds." Aragon's narrator commented: "The hope of revolution rises upon words that pile into a tower of eloquence. Dancing words, sounds, like bullets, fraught with death. The ideas are like songs in the cathedral of Basel."[14]

The International Socialist Bureau became the driving force in the struggle for peace. But the eloquence of Jaurès and other orators should not obscure the fact that the Extraordinary Ninth Conference was another failure. Five hundred fifty representatives from twenty-three countries agreed that war would be a catastrophe, but once again, they could not agree on how to prevent it. Some recommended a general strike, which others thought impossible because of national imperatives.

At the time, European socialist parties represented major political forces. After the 1912 elections the SPD had become the largest political party in Germany, with 110 deputies. However, the party contained very different groups: reformists, Marxists, and left-wingers. Their differences made it difficult to undertake any common action in response to the danger of war. German socialists, like their French comrades, denounced the "arms race" and the militaristic turn, but many of them remained convinced of the legitimacy of national defense and of the goodwill of the German government toward preserving peace.

August Bebel, who died in 1913, embodied all of these contradictions. The great German socialist leader thought that a general international strike in case of war was not possible. Instead, he preferred to reach out to the government of Chancellor Bethmann-Hollweg, in order to encourage an accord with Great Britain. During the Agadir Crisis of 1911, Bebel addressed the dangers of a future war, in a speech with eschatological overtones: "Thus arms will be taken up on all sides and we will reach a point where one or another of the adversaries will say: 'Better a swift and horrible end than endless horror.' This is the moment when catastrophe will strike. All Europe will follow the drumbeats, and sixteen to eighteen million men in the flower of their youth, the best men from the different nations, will go to war equipped with the best instruments of assassination."

In France, tensions within the left-wing political parties reached their breaking point during the debate over the Three-Years Law, which divided the country during spring and summer 1913. It seemed that the bitterness of the Dreyfus Affair twenty years earlier had resurfaced. In 1905, a law was passed reducing active military service from three to two years. Military officers had opposed this change, because they thought that the law weakened national defense. In fact, the law of 1905 had also canceled the exemptions specified in the military law of 1889: at that time, men training for the priesthood, those with large families, and university students were excused from military service. Canceling these exemptions meant that the army regained seventy-two thousand men and could maintain its numbers at a constant level. Following the resurgence of Franco-German tensions, the issue was now whether to restore the requirement of three years of active military service.

The French Parliament began discussions on the subject in March 1913 and adopted Plan XVII the next month. This new plan for military operations in case of war had a more offensive focus. President Raymond Poincaré, elected on January 17, 1913, placed great importance on the alliance with Russia. In his eyes, the best way to reassure his allies of the readiness of the French military was to increase the length of active military service. This reform was part of a broader context of rethinking the mission of the French army and what strategy it should adopt in case of conflict. Here we find the viewpoint developed by French socialists and in particular their leader, Jean Jaurès.

Published in 1911, Jaurès's book *The New Army* discussed his proposed bill on the organization of the army. This was an important work because of its historical references and its depth: like Clausewitz, Jaurès thought that war and politics could not be separated; like Marx, he thought that social forces were the determining historical forces. It was also an important book because it did not address military issues alone. "It is through questions relative to national defense and international peace that I discuss the Socialist plan of organization for France, which I wish to present to Parliament in legislative terms." In fact, *The New Army* was meant to be the first in a series of works, a vast intellectual project that was brutally cut short by Jaurès's assassination on July 31, 1914.

Why begin with military reform in order to make the progressive, nonviolent transition toward the socialist society Jaurès wished for? Doubtless because "the problem of France's military organization is that in appearance, it is a nation in arms and in reality it is not, or just barely," he wrote. The law of 1889 had created a contingent of 600,000 men. It also created a large officer corps cut off from the rest of society and often hostile to the republican government.

Jaurès was no less critical of the law of March 1905, which reduced military service to two years without reorganizing the army reserves, to which every citizen belonged for eleven years after the end of his active military service. For him, the weakness of the army reserves not only endangered the country in the event of German aggression but also betrayed the very function of an army in a republic: the army represents the nation in arms, and as such, it embodies the indissoluble link between citizenship and conscription. To reorganize the reserves would allow for the personal engagement of citizens in the defense of their country beyond active military service. By making a massive mobilization possible in case of war, the reform would also have a dissuasive effect on an adversary.

Jaurès did not have long to wait for the antimilitarist left's criticisms of *The New Army*. The official newspaper of the General Confederation of Labor (CGT) deplored the return of *bataillons scolaires*, units that were attached to a lycée, middle school, or primary school and initiated students to military training. Military reform would be nothing other than "the most ingenious system for one class to militarily subjugate another." In military circles, the book was greeted with curiosity, and sometimes even with admiration for the author's erudition, concern for national defense, and ability to compromise, which set him apart from other Socialists. But the book was certainly more discussed than actually read.

On March 6, 1913, Minister of War Eugène Étienne took the floor in the Chamber of Deputies and defended the proposed law. The atmosphere was electric. Gathered around Jaurès, the Socialist deputies were furious at the idea of military reform, presented almost out of the blue. They were even more furious when the minister explained that the proposal was merely "a permanent application" of the exceptions to the law of 1905; this law already authorized the government to keep men in their last year of military service in the army, in case of imminent war. But did this risk really exist in 1913?

In the 1920s and 1930s, when people attempted to assign responsibility for the First World War, the Three-Years Law was sometimes viewed as a reaction to a project increasing the size of the German army. In reality, the French proposal was presented to the deputies on March 6, whereas the German proposal was put forth on March 29 and discussed in the Reichstag only at the beginning of April.[15] With hindsight, the specific chronology regarding new laws on military service seems less important than the climate of fear that prevailed at this time: the Germans' fear of finding themselves surrounded by the coalition of Russia, France, and Great Britain; the French fear of German militarism and demographic power (sixty-seven million Germans versus forty-one million

French in 1914); the fear in every European country of being militarily and economically surpassed by other countries.

For example, Kaiser Wilhelm II declared in a telegram to his ambassador in St. Petersburg on July 30, 1914: "For I have no doubt left about it: England, Russia and France have *agreed* among themselves . . . to take the Austro-Serbian conflict for an *excuse* for waging a *war of extermination* against us. . . . So the famous '*encirclement*' of Germany has finally become a complete fact, despite every effort of our politicians and diplomats to prevent it. The net has been suddenly thrown over our head, and England sneeringly reaps the most brilliant success of her persistently prosecuted purely *anti-German world-policy*, against which we have proved ourselves helpless, while she twists the noose of our political and economic destruction out of our fidelity to Austria, as we squirm *isolated* in the net."[16]

In France, supporters of the Three-Years Law also felt this vague anxiety. They all asserted that it was a question not of a "law of aggression, of provocation" but of a defensive law: "a question of life or death," as Louis Barthou, the président du Conseil since March 22, 1913, explained. In the face of danger, a solid army of conscripts was needed. It was thought that the first battles would be violent and swift, leaving hardly any time to call up the reserves.[17] In an article published in the *Revue des Deux Mondes*, Major Patrice Mahon predicted that the German army had become "a shock army," ready to attack France.[18]

This fear of German aggression had a name—*l'attaque brusquée*—that military experts and journalists used regularly in the years preceding the war. In military language, this term refers to an unexpected attack in a specific sector, but in 1913 many French envisioned the 822,000 soldiers of the German army surging out of the blue across the borders of north and northeastern France. In consequence, many French strategists had an almost religious obsession with the need for the *offensive à outrance*. No matter that the Russo-Japanese War, or more recently, the Balkan Wars, had proved the futility of such attacks in the face of modern weapons and their deluge of firepower. A defensive strategy was thought to be tactically inferior to an offensive strategy, and above all, morally inferior.

Those opposed to the law, on the contrary, thought a surprise attack by the Germans was impossible. They insisted on the role of the reserves, which they saw as essential to any modern army. In their view, a reservist is more aware of what he is defending than a conscript. Jaurès, their leader, was soon the target of violent attacks in the Chamber of Deputies and in the press. The cover of the illustrated supplement to *Le Petit Journal* depicts an angry Marianne lecturing him, reminding him of the crimes committed by the Prussians during the war of 1870–71. The drawing was captioned: "Remember, then." Caricatures portrayed him as a small, obese man wearing a spiked helmet. For those in favor of the law, it was clear that the Socialist leader was playing Germany's game. "Once again we find him working hard against France's interests in favor of his party," wrote André Tardieu, the editor in chief of international affairs for the newspaper *Le Temps*. "For ten years now, in every crisis he has been against national interests and for foreigners. Today he is exactly where we vigilantly expected him, standing against national duty."[19] One of Jaurès's most violent attackers, as we have seen, was Charles

Péguy, doubtless because he had admired Jaurès at the time of the Dreyfus Affair and now felt betrayed. In a two-part article entitled "L'Argent" (On money) and published in the *Cahiers de la quinzaine* in April 1913, he stigmatized those intellectuals who opposed the law and who had formed a group, led by Lucien Herr, the legendary head librarian of the École normale supérieure: "The Prussian army is perhaps their adversary, but the French army is certainly their enemy."[20]

It would be wrong, however, to draw hasty conclusions from the climate of hatred that prevailed when the law was voted on. Although the debates might recall the Dreyfus Affair due to their violence, they lasted only for several months; the Affair had divided France for more than ten years. In 1913, war was thought to be imminent; a year later, tensions had fallen. Many thought that a new crisis in the Balkans would not be of any greater consequence than the Moroccan crises of 1905 and 1911. Hence the relative lack of interest in France regarding the news of the assassination of an Austro-Hungarian archduke and his wife in Sarajevo on June 28, 1914. At the time, public opinion was much more preoccupied with the trial of Henriette Caillaux, the second wife of the former président du Conseil, Joseph Caillaux. She had assassinated the editor-in-chief of the newspaper *Le Figaro*, Gaston Calmette, to avenge the press campaign against her husband.[21] In Roger Martin du Gard's multivolume novel *Les Thibault*, set during the first two decades of the twentieth century, the Socialist Jacques Thibault laments: "Accounts of Madame Caillaux's trial took up the entire first page of almost every daily newspaper. ... Most newspapers courteously stated their confidence in Germany, which, during the Balkan crisis had always shown itself able to counsel moderation to its Austrian ally."[22] Although the question of Alsace-Lorraine had inspired much fervor after the war of 1870–71, it no longer seemed to matter. In classrooms, maps of France still bore black borders, mourning for the lost provinces. But in public opinion, reclaiming Alsace-Lorraine was no longer a reason to go to war.

Finally, the nationalist rise of 1913—a renewed nationalism on the right as well as on the left—was not apparent in the election results of April–May 1914. During the second round of voting, the right lost twenty-six seats; the Socialists gained thirty, and the radicals hostile to the law also gained thirty.[23] The left-wing parties hostile to the law won the day. With the new national assembly, it seemed certain that the law would be abrogated the following autumn. The declaration of war would decide otherwise.

UNION SACRÉE

The two opposing groups in the Chamber of Deputies did have one thing in common: their deep-seated patriotism. Part of the left was hostile to the law and had warned that in case of war, they would call for a strike, under certain conditions, but they considered themselves to be as patriotic as their adversaries. They did not rule out defending the country against outside aggression.[24] The antimilitarist left, on the other hand, openly proclaimed both its hostility to the army and its goal to oppose war at any cost. How would they react at the moment of mobilization? Would there be strikes, rebellions, insubordination, desertion, sabotage?

These were pressing questions. In the last days of July 1914, opposition to the war had broken out in areas where the labor movement was strong: in the provinces, mainly industrial regions, and in Paris.[25] In Montluçon, in central France, a major demonstration rallied nearly ten thousand people on July 30, 1914; it was the largest such demonstration. In Sotteville, an industrial suburb of Rouen, the railway workers organized at the end of the workday, shouting "Vive la paix!" In the small industrial region of Vimeu, in Picardy, several hundreds of metalworkers headed for the labor exchange in Escarbotin, shouting "Down with war!" and "War on war!" In Paris, demonstrations were organized on the Grands Boulevards. Thousands of people answered the unions' call. Clashes between the police and demonstrators took place on July 27 on the Boulevard Poissonnière: "Broken canes, hats, and caps strew the sidewalks and the road; on several benches, numerous overcoats and umbrellas could be seen, watched over by the police . . ."[26]

Such incidents made disorder and sabotage seem likely if war were declared. Since 1909, a nationwide file created in 1886 to fight espionage had tracked antimilitary union members and activists thought likely to engage in subversive action. It was called the Carnet B to distinguish it from the Carnet A, which listed the names of foreigners old enough to bear arms. These files, relayed to departmental gendarmeries, were meant to allow for activists to be arrested as soon as mobilization was decreed. Few Socialist leaders were on this list, with the exception of Gustave Hervé, known for his strong antimilitarist position. Also named was of one of his close friends, Aristide Jobert (who became a deputy for the

Yonne in 1914), as well as local Socialist activists, and especially many anarchists who belonged to the labor movement. What is striking is the disproportion between the fears that the Carnet B stirred up (the shadowy existence of organized groups ready to use violence to stop the mobilization) and the reality: there was no major plan of action, no cache of arms, no coordinated or trained movement. Significantly, the président du Conseil, René Viviani, and the minister of the interior, Louis Malvy, had decided during the night of July 31–August 1, 1914, to refrain from using the Carnet B. They did so against the advice of the minister of war, Adolphe Messimy, the same man who a few days later would say, "Give me the guillotine and I'll guarantee you victory!"

The preventive security measures long since prepared were abandoned the very morning that the mobilization was announced. What happened? The answer lies in the attitude of the French labor movement in response to the last stages of the July Crisis. The general mobilization in Serbia occurred on July 25; Austria-Hungary declared war on Serbia on the twenty-eighth and bombed Belgrade on the twenty-ninth. The Russians announced a partial mobilization at noon on the twenty-ninth, canceled it at 10 PM after an exchange of telegrams between Kaiser Wilhelm II and Czar Nicholas II, and then confirmed the mobilization the next day. On the evening of the twenty-ninth, the International Socialist Bureau held an urgent meeting in Brussels, giving Jaurès a triumphal welcome in the great room of the Cirque Royal. On July 30, President Poincaré, who had come back to France from his trip to Russia the day before, decided to have the initial covering force deployed to the border. And then there was an astonishing series

of new developments on the last day of peace, July 31, hour by
hour. Berlin proclaimed a *Kriegsgefahrzustand* (threatening
danger of war) at 1:45 PM, followed by an ultimatum to Russia
and France. Then came the order for general mobilization in
Austria-Hungary and the completion of the French frontier
covering force at 5:40 PM. Belgium declared a general mobilization at 7 PM. The undersecretary of state for foreign affairs,
Abel Ferry, welcomed back Jaurès and the French socialist
delegation—at the very moment when Viviani was meeting
the German ambassador Wilhelm von Schoen.

Faced with this rapid series of events during the last days
of July 1914, labor groups had ceased their opposition. It was
necessary to keep pressure on the government to fight for
peace: such was the meaning of the demonstrations in Paris
on July 27. German activists had the same attitude toward
their own government. If war were to break out, however, it
was unthinkable for French and German socialists to lead
their respective countries to military defeat. The Socialists
were pacifists, but certainly not defeatists. Jaurès had always
made it clear that he valued national defense. Karl Marx's
famous phrase, "the proletariat has no country," made him
indignant. Moreover, the declarations of war in August 1914
would prove Marx wrong: all across Europe, the proletariat
joined various national armies not due to the force of circumstances but out of a patriotic reflex to defend their country.

When the International Socialist Bureau had met in
Brussels on July 29, Jaurès reiterated his confidence in the
French government's policy of "peace through arbitration."
The delegates made one decision: to move up the date of
their international congress, holding it in Paris on August 9

instead of in Vienna on August 23. "None of us who were there thought to ask what we would do if war broke out before the congress," Karl Kautsky recalled several years later. "What position should socialist parties take in this war?" In the interwar period, the Communists severely criticized the labor movement's lack of response on the eve of the conflict: why had the Second International failed? Why had the promises of peace made to left-wing activists been betrayed?[27]

French socialists were overcome by a growing pessimism, as dramatic news reached them from abroad. Did Jaurès still believe in the chances for peace on July 31, when he met with Abel Ferry at the end of the afternoon? Did he think he could negotiate Socialist support for a strictly defensive war? All hopes for solidarity with German social democrats were destroyed when he was assassinated. France, and left-wing activists in particular, were at a loss. Many of them felt like the Carmaux miners whom he represented, "demoralized, disconcerted, despairing."[28] It seemed clear that nothing more could stop war from breaking out. The young novelist Louis Pergaud wrote in a letter on August 1, "With the death of the great citizen who was truly the best of men, and the most enlightened of patriots, also dies one of the best advisers of the people of France and one of the most vigilant defenders of peace in the world."[29] In his journal of the war years, the writer Romain Rolland seems to take a somewhat colder attitude: "Saturday, August 1. This morning, heard about Jaurès's assassination. . . . A great thinker, a generous heart; I admired him all while having for him a unique mix of sympathy . . . and antipathy."[30]

In the provinces, however, Jaurès's death inspired less emotion than it did in Paris, except in those regions with strong left-wing tradition. Some local newspapers found out about the assassination too late to discuss it in detail in their August 1 editions. August 2 was a Sunday. By August 3, the general mobilization had become top priority. For the immense majority of the French population, time passed differently than it did for diplomats and chiefs of state. Too busy with the harvest, too distant from political debates and news on the international crisis, the inhabitants of the countryside (who numbered more than half the population) had learned nothing of the gravity of the situation. In several days, surprise changed into a kind of firm resolve, almost instinctive, mixing patriotic convictions and a defensive reaction.[31]

Several things were now clear. The war was here; it was a fact. Collective fervor, the force of circumstances, the legal obligation to bear arms, and fear of the firing squad left no choice. And so the number of deserters and rebels was almost negligible, less than one percent of those mobilized in France.[32] That said, the fact that antimilitarist socialists and revolutionary labor movement activists fought in the war should not make us forget that they did so at the cost of a painful crisis of conscience. They had to renounce their other battle, no doubt partially and provisionally. They recognized their powerlessness in the face of circumstances, and hoped for a short war. They mourned Jaurès, whose memory was immediately used by Viviani on August 1 to justify "the patriotic action of his government."

Consider the correspondence and private notebooks of activists. After leaving a meeting of his local Socialist group on the evening of July 31, a young Parisian wrote that the European war on the horizon was like "something immense and barbaric that disconcerts us, that disarms us and makes us seem like pygmies. . . . What happened to all the declarations that had been made? Where are the threats: general strike, insurrection? We feel caught up in the storm as if we were being squeezed by a vise. It carries you off and immobilizes you. We are speechless, anguished, disoriented."[33]

At first resigned, then determined to defend their country, many had the feeling that the threat of war had been weighing on them for too long, but that it was time to get on with it, once and for all. A Union sacrée was established between the leaders of the various political parties by the beginning of August. "Union sacrée": the expression had strength and solemnity. It even had a religious dimension, which did not escape the legislators listening to a message from Poincaré that Viviani read to Parliament on August 4, 1914. Those present stood and remained standing while the président du Conseil delivered the president of the Republic's message. It ran, in part, "In the war that is beginning, France will have Right on her side, the eternal power of which cannot with impunity be disregarded by nations any more than by individuals." Loud and unanimous applause followed this statement, according to the *Journal officiel*. "She will be heroically defended by all her sons: nothing will break their Union sacrée before the enemy: to-day they are joined together as brothers in a common indignation against the aggressor, and in a common patriotic faith." This sentence was met with "loud and prolonged applause and cries of 'Vive la France.' "[34]

In reality, a better term would have been "political truce." When war was declared, an ideological cease-fire characterized political life. Many thought this reprieve would be as provisional as the war would be short-lived. The tensions that had surrounded the debate over the Three-Years Law disappeared with this new and somewhat forced unanimity. The elderly Socialist Édouard Vaillant, seventy-four years old and a veteran of the Commune of 1871, had previously supported the idea of a general strike in case of war; now he declared, "In the presence of aggression, the Socialists will fulfill their duty to the country, to the Republic, to the Socialist International."

At Jaurès's funeral, held on the morning of August 4, the political truce seemed almost tangible. A catafalque had been constructed at the corner of avenue Henri Martin and rue de la Pompe, near the late Socialist leader's Paris residence. A crowd had enveloped the street since the early morning. All the Socialist deputies were there, and several government ministers accompanied Viviani. The leaders of the CGT were present, along with representatives from the international Socialist Bureau, such as the Belgian deputy Camille Huysmans, but so, too, were conservative deputies. All came together for one of the great and solemn state burials of the Third Republic.

Léon Jouhaux, the secretary general of the CGT, gave a moving speech that exemplified how the pacifist left mourned its hopes of peace. This speech was a powerful symbol of the political truce necessitated by the declaration of war: "Jaurès was our comfort in our impassioned work for peace. It is not his fault nor ours if peace has not triumphed. It is war that has arisen. Before heading toward the great massacre, in the name of all the workers who have left, and in the name of all those who will leave and among whom I count myself, I cry aloud before this coffin all our hatred of savage imperialism, which

brings forth the horrible crime [of war]." The labor movement would not oppose the mobilization. It would bend to
the requirements of national defense, in the name of patriotic
Jacobinism and hatred of German militarism.

Pacifist activists had not really given up. Some continued
to hope that the war would bring the end of imperialism,
even the revolution. For a part of the French left, however,
supporting the policy of national defense continued to be a
painful choice, along with the fact that Socialists Jules Guesde
and Marcel Sembat had joined the Viviani government on
August 26. Some never completely accepted the new reality.
In a country at war, however, dissident voices are quickly
silenced.

The photographs taken in train stations during the first days of
August seem to show a feeling of enthusiasm, the illusion of a
departure "la fleur au fusil." The great historian of Catholicism
André Latreille was among the first to criticize this illusion on
the occasion of the fiftieth anniversary of the declaration of
war; he was thirteen years old in 1914: "Certainly, there were
some noisy demonstrations in Paris on the boulevards, and perhaps in some of the trains full of mobilized men. In the major
newspapers, there were articles in a heroic tone whose unbearable optimism is striking today. It might be tempting to use
some photos from the *Miroir* and some excerpts from *Le Matin*
and *L'Écho de Paris* to sketch out a picture of public opinion, but
this would be completely erroneous. In the country as a whole,
for the immense majority of French men and women affected
and separated by the mobilization, the dominant tone was quite
different: grave resignation and general anxiety."[35]

The historian Jean-Jacques Becker has analyzed the reports on public response to the mobilization, written by schoolteachers in the Dauphiné at the initiative of the historian Charles Petit-Dutaillis, who in 1914 was head of the Grenoble school district. Becker has also analyzed the reports of teachers from other regions, which has led him to question the myth of an enthusiastic departure for the front. "Doing your duty did not mean that you had been brutally converted to a noisy nationalism."[36] How did people react to an event so long anticipated and imagined—by the general staff, Socialist activists, novelists, and journalists? How did they react when the object of so many fears became reality in the summer of 1914, paradoxically taking public opinion by surprise? An important witness from this time, the great medievalist Marc Bloch, best described the ambivalence of French reactions: "The sadness that was buried in our hearts showed only in the red and swollen eyes of many women. Out of the specter of war, the nation's armies created a sense of democratic fervor. ... On the streets, in the stores and streetcars, strangers chatted freely; the unanimous goodwill, though often expressed in naïve or awkward words and gestures, was nonetheless moving. The men for the most part were not hearty; they were resolute, and that was better."[37]

CHAPTER THREE

Farewell Ceremonies

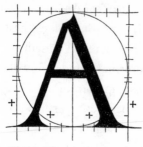

LL over France, civilians and soldiers bade each other goodbye; the
first wave of mobilized men numbered nearly 3,781,000. In the
months and years that followed,
another four million French soldiers
left home. The American painter
Albert Herter created a mural of this poignant moment, entitled *The Departure of the Infantrymen*. Measuring sixteen feet
high by forty feet long, it has hung in the departure hall of the
Gare de l'Est in Paris since 1926, when Herter presented the
painting to the French Railway Company. Marshal Joffre at-
tended the ceremony.

In the center, a soldier stands on the footboard of a train
ready to leave for the front; the soldier's face is that of Everit
Albert Herter, the painter's son. A student at Harvard University and an artist himself, Everit did not join the American

army until September 1917. His father's mural purposely combines the period when France entered the war with the period when the United States did. It is as if Albert Herter seeks to represent two countries united in the same sacred cause, as well as his family's personal connection to France. Everit and his brother Christian Archibald Herter (who in spring 1917 was an attaché to the American ambassador in Berlin) had spent part of their childhood in Europe, accompanied by their parents, and completed their secondary schooling in France.[1]

In the painting, Everit Herter looks skyward. A handful of flowers pokes out of the barrel of his gun—an allusion to the supposed French attitude in early August 1914. However, neither the certainty of a short war nor the conviction of a just one dominates the composition. Numerous soldiers crowd around the young man, and yet he seems somewhat apart from them: there is a sort of halo above his head, reflected in the whiteness of his shirt. His arms stretch out and his body evokes a cross. All of this perhaps suggests the deeper meaning of the image; rather than celebrate the soldiers' departure, it alludes to the almost Christlike sacrifice awaiting an entire generation. Other soldiers in sky-blue uniforms put their luggage away. A seated young man seems lost in thought.

To show the individual dimensions of this collective experience, Herter depicts three generations mingling on the platform. Many soldiers are accompanied by their families, although in reality civilians had to remain outside the train station. A couple is locked in a close embrace, while their son clings to his mother's skirt. A soldier kneels on the ground, holding his children tightly. Another holds an infant who is still wearing a newborn's cap. Sitting on a suitcase, an old man weeps. His wife tries in vain to console him. Other families have brought bottles of wine, some bread, and other provisions for the trip. The soldiers' red trousers stand out against the dominant blue and gray tones that characterize their families' clothing. The uniform makes the soldier; it visually and symbolically separates the draftees from the rest of society, and signals the particular fate of the man wearing it. Some were called to go to the front lines right away, while others were condemned to wait and count the days.[2]

A bouquet in his hand, Albert Herter stands among the civilians. So does his wife, the artist Adele McGinnis Herter. Their faces are those of an elderly couple, even though in 1914 they were only in their forties. Adele stands opposite her husband, clothed in white, wrapped in a shawl, her hands joined as if in prayer. These gestures of mourning—the bouquet that will be placed at a grave and the prayer for the departed—announce the catastrophe that will befall the Herter family and millions of others. In this painting, Albert Herter captured a decisive moment in modern French history and in his own life. Everit volunteered to join a camouflage section; he was killed in June 1918.[3]

THE SLOW HOURS

During the first days of August 1914, similar scenes of farewell were taking place all across France. Zacharie Baqué was a schoolteacher in the small village of Vic-Fezensac in southwest France. On Saturday, August 1, the entire village had gathered in the main square, expecting news. At five o'clock in the afternoon, the postmaster's wife went out to meet the crowd, her eyes red from crying. Several minutes later, the tocsin rang out. Zacharie then went home on foot to the hamlet of Les Ormeaux, where he lived with his family: his wife, daughter, mother, grandmother, and aunt. On his way, he ran into a neighbor: "Where's the fire?" she asked, pretending that this was the reason the bells were ringing. "At the border!" he replied. Two days later, he left home at dawn. He had to arrive at the barracks of the 88th Infantry Regiment by the third day of the mobilization. "Anguished farewells . . .," he noted soberly in his diary. A neighbor took him to the train station at Jegun, about twelve miles away. From there he took the train to Auch, and then Mirande, about another twenty-five miles.[4] In the countryside, people said goodbye at the front doors of their homes, or in the village square. The draftees who had to report on the first day kept each other's morale up with jokes and bragging. The barrelmaker Louis Barthas, from Peyriac-Minervois in the south of France, remembered it this way: "On August 4, the third day of mobilization, about half the mobilized men of the village embarked at the train station, accompanied by almost the whole population."[5]

Monotony, rather than the fear of the war, prevailed during the first days of the mobilization. "My impressions of life in the barracks? It smells bad, the meat is tough, and we're bored," noted Roland Dorgelès.[6] From Albi, in the southwest, where he had rejoined his regiment, Henri Barbusse wrote a letter to his wife: in the barracks, "exactly the same memories arise, on top of the ones from twenty years ago" when he performed his military service. "It's the same habits, the same jokes, the same smells."[7] The men rediscovered the lack of privacy and comfort, and the strict discipline that made them realize that if they were not yet in active combat, they weren't quite civilians any longer either. "We miss our cider, and that doesn't help," complained the gunner Alexandre, from the village of Colomby, in Normandy.[8]

The mobilization had quadrupled the size of the armed forces in the space of a few days. Garrison towns were quickly overcome by the sheer numbers of mobilized men. In Brest, they were housed in elementary schools and the high school. In Marmande, a small southwestern city of narrow streets, Jacques Rivière, then an assistant editor of *La Nouvelle Revue française*, was struck by how the city swelled in size with the several thousand soldiers it now lodged, stuck in an "endless and exasperating" wait: "Slow hours. . . . Everything before us looks vague and empty. . . . No one is hurried. All feverishness is gone. I don't think about the war anymore. I feel again that wretched sadness of empty hours in the barracks. All these men who don't know each other, sitting there together, no one knows why anymore, with their bundles wrapped in a colored kerchief. When the quartermaster comes to talk to us about the war, I say to myself: Hey! It's true!" Every evening, the restaurants were full of people—soldiers in the regular army, with their blue kepi covers, soldiers from the Territorial Army, many men at loose ends, drinking, playing cards, and insulting the Germans. Rivière took refuge in the room he had rented in the city, describing its "delicious feeling" of solitude, accentuated by the back and forth of heavily booted men passing in the street.

Before the local regiments were to leave, a final parade took place. In Cherbourg, in the northwest, the people gathered in the early afternoon of August 7, under an icy wind, at place Divette. The regimental band arrived, followed by the troops marching in close ranks, with fixed bayonets. All along the parade route, residents threw flowers from their windows. Men attached them to their uniforms or to their gun barrels. In Pamiers, in the southwest, the 59th Infantry Regiment left the city "to the sound of enthusiastic acclaim."[9] In Montluçon, one of the first cities to elect a Socialist mayor, a heavy crowd had accompanied the 121st Infantry Regiment to the train station. The area's local deputy and sous-préfet marched at the head of the procession.[10] These events followed the tradition of the patriotic parades for July 14: flags representing the regiment's history and identity; songs and speeches; raising the colors on the parade ground. But this time, high spirits arose in the context of going to war, and the oft-repeated rituals took on a unique feeling. The troops' route was lengthened so that they could go through all the main neighborhoods of the city. After the individual farewells to families, the civic community bade farewell to its soldiers.

At the end of the Great War, local authorities could not help but think back to these ceremonies of 1914 in their speeches welcoming the demobilized soldiers home. In 1918–19, soldiers returning from the front defined themselves as survivors of the summer 1914 cohort, even if in the end there weren't many of them. "I will never forget the nights of August 1914 when the city came to the train station to say farewell to our regiments from the Vendée, the 93rd, the 83rd, and the 293rd. No, I will never be able to forget the departures of those soldiers so full of spirit and enthusiasm. What became of those brilliant officers, those valiant privates who so bravely left to fight a hereditary enemy?" wondered a deputy mayor in La Roche-sur-Yon in the Vendée, on September 21, 1919. "Alas! How many fell gloriously on the field of battle? How many remain on the fields of the Marne, in Hébuterne [a destroyed village in the Pas-de-Calais], and in the many other battles where the regiment distinguished itself?"

The memory of "the men of '14" would be in people's minds during the welcome home ceremonies. Indeed, victory celebrations reproduced, in reverse fashion, the rituals of departure. When the last soldiers had returned to their cities of origin, the older men, who had been demobilized first, went to meet their fellow soldiers at the same train stations they had left from five years earlier. Together they crossed the city, preceded by their regimental flag, as if the cycle of war was closing behind them. In Quimper, Brittany, the city organized a reception in honor of the 118th Infantry Regiment on September 14, 1919; all the survivors had returned by September 9. Train stations were a threshold in both directions, toward the front lines and the home front, between peacetime and war.[11]

DIGNITY AND RESOLVE

"On August 1, all of France became a train station. Each hill sheltered a railway line; each village was a stop along the way."[12] All along their various routes, trains had been decorated with flowers and greenery given by locals. In Bourges, a child had written in chalk on a locomotive: "Excursion train, Bourges–Berlin, round trip." Others had drawn caricatures of the kaiser, but with a chamber pot for a helmet.[13] In the hot days that followed, mobilized men traveled all across France.

Ten thousand trains had been requisitioned, five thousand for the concentration phase of operations alone. In their stories, the mobilized men describe their journey as a progressive distancing from their region of origin and as a patriotic initiation into the reality of France at war. At each step of the journey, a welcoming committee and crowds acclaimed the soldiers.

And so the gunner Ivan Cassagnau left the southwest, his home region, to head to the Vosges sector in the northeast. When he arrived in Heiwiller, near Belfort, he began to keep a diary, and continued to do so until he was wounded at Verdun in April 1916. "How far away it is already, that fatal date of August 2! And yet how close it still is!" he wrote, a mere three weeks after the mobilization. "On August 2, my life was ripped apart. Until then, I was leading a happy life. I didn't know it, but I realize it now. Since that day, I have known more worries, anguish, pain, and mourning than in all of my twenty-four years." This young man would soon know combat for the first time. On August 19 alone, 2 officers, 8 non-commissioned officers, and 117 of his comrades were killed or declared missing. The French 75mm field guns also decimated the enemy infantry. Then Cassagnau returns to his retrospective account of his journey to the frontlines: "August 10, departure effective 3:30 for an unknown destination. Sleep! No one can think about that. . . . At Narbonne, the locals spoil us. Wine was freely and copiously distributed. At Sète, we were given some beautiful apples. We gaze at the sea, which a lot of the men have never seen. . . . At Valence, ladies of the Red Cross circulate all along the convoy, giving us coffee, chocolate, sandwiches, and cigarettes. The city is foggy. Later, we reach Besançon and the Jura, where the fields are so green it surprises us. Back home, at this time of year, the fields are baked."[14] Mobilization was first of all a journey, a kind of odyssey.

Other regiments went via Paris, before spreading out to various destinations in the east of France. By their very monumentality, all the Paris train stations seemed destined to set the stage for the mobilization, with their moving crowds, collective emotions, and massive presence of adult men, such as France had never before seen in the modern era. According to historian Adrian Gregory, "Train stations shape war, just as they have already shaped cities."[15] In the space of a few days, hundreds of thousands of travelers crossed paths. These gateways of the modern city became symbolic thresholds to war. The first groups of mobilized men left for the concentration zone and for the borders; others hurriedly went to Paris barracks. Civilians from Belgium and the north of France fled the threat of German invasion. Parisians sought to leave the capital, while foreigners were trapped by the declaration of war. Ordinary individuals who had come to Paris for work or for the summer left for their home region, in order to join their unit or to take shelter.

The Gare de Montparnasse and the Gare d'Austerlitz welcomed the masses that had been mobilized in the south of France, who in their turn encountered civilians fleeing the war. Men from the Rhône Valley, Provence, and the Massif Central arrived at the Gare de Lyon. Buses and taxis requisitioned by the army took them to the Gare de l'Est and the Gare du Nord, where they met up with soldiers from the Paris region and with crowds of family, friends, and those who were simply curious. The Gare du Nord served as the departure point for all soldiers heading to Lille, Arras, Saint-Quentin, Dunkerque, and Laon. Among them was the historian Marc Bloch, who was teaching at a high school in Amiens; he left Paris on August 4, 1914, to join the 272nd Infantry Regiment.

Cars carrying mobilized men had a difficult time making their way through the crowd in front of the Gare de l'Est, which served Verdun, Nancy, and Belfort. On August 2, reservists arrived, carrying bundles filled with food; that morning, they had received their individual call-up orders in the mail. The professional photographer Jacques Moreau, aged twenty-seven in 1914, took photos all over the neighborhoods surrounding the train stations before leaving for the front himself. His photographs—a little more than two thousand small-sized glass plates—constitute the best eyewitness account of an urban space gripped by war: streams of soldiers marching with Lebel rifles on their shoulders while crowds of civilians greet them. The weather was hot and stormy. Some soldiers had unbuttoned the necks of their uniforms while they waited, sitting on the ground, in the shadow of the plane trees lining the avenues. As they drew closer to the station, they became quieter.

And so this wave of humanity slowly progressed toward the Gare de l'Est. At the top of the building, Lemaire's sculpture depicting the city of Strasbourg seemed to promise the recapture of Alsace-Lorraine, which was not, however, one of the reasons for going to war in 1914. The gates of the great courtyard, in front of the departure hall, had been closed to keep civilians out. To reach the platforms, a soldier had to show his papers to a guard from the Territorial Army, and then enter via a small door at the left of the building. The travelers who were trying to leave Paris—Belgians, but in the first hours of the mobilization, Germans as well—went via the door on the right.

The youngest among the mobilized men entered the station quickly, without turning around, often in groups of two or three. In photographs, they look insouciant, as if bantering with one another. Perhaps the presence of fellow soldiers inspired them to put on a cheerful front. A reporter from the *Petit Journal* was struck by their resolve and patriotism: "Smiling and proud almost to a man, they gathered in the courtyard before heading to the waiting rooms, like bands of brothers."[16] Those who had come with their families, including children and elderly relatives, seemed the most somber. Their farewells took place in front of the gates. This was where the war began, with its separation, its waiting, its worries. When a mobilized man disappeared inside the train station, as if carried off by the wave of collective destiny, he no longer belonged to civilian society. Women and children would then stay for a moment, hands gripping the bars of the gate, wearing expressions of intense sadness, as the tight framing of Moreau's photographs reveals. They were peering at the crowd of uniforms, trying to catch one last glimpse of their loved ones.

Numerous rituals take place when a country goes to war: parades, farewell speeches, various ceremonies, and the roll-out of all kinds of patriotic insignia—flags, banners, rosettes, pennants, and standards. For several days, and often for several weeks, the mobilized men would increasingly shed their civilian identity in order to become soldiers. The rituals were in place to encourage this transition, through both their collective nature (the men were never alone; they belonged to an age group, a regiment, a civic community) and their performative one (the ceremonies made the soldier; they reminded him of what he ought to be in order to meet the expectations of his country, of society, and of his family).

For there was not just one threshold to cross, but an entire series of successive steps from peacetime to wartime. Leaving home was the first decisive moment—a private ritual, even if it often took place in a public space. Next were the farewells at the train station, with the moving crowds, the shouts mixing with the puffing of the locomotive, the carriages bearing flowers and greenery. Then came the baptism by fire itself, which all the witness accounts describe. The men then truly experienced war. They saw destroyed houses and heard shelling in the distance; they beheld dead bodies (those of men and horses) for the first time. They spent their first nights in the trenches and they fought their first battles. At this stage, their farewell to civilian life must have seemed far away.

In addition to these formal rituals, emotional intensity made this experience an exceptional moment. Nothing can be compared to leaving for war: anguish and the fear of death grip the hearts of those saying goodbye. This collective departure became deeply inscribed in the memory of those who experienced it and in several generations of the collective memory. The film producer and director Abel Gance captured the essence of these farewells in *J'accuse*, an important film he shot in 1918–19. In the opening scenes, Gance used numerous nonprofessional actors, many of whom had been demobilized several weeks earlier. In a Provençal village in summer 1914, a group of peasants gathers to dance a farandole and celebrate the Saint-Jean, or Midsummer. The villagers seem joyful, heady with music and wine. The dancing spills out onto the streets, and the setting sun casts the dancers' shadows on the walls. Suddenly, the dancing stops. Someone has found an owl at the door of a farm. Its eyes, filmed in close-up, in the shadows, are fixed on the dancers. Everyone vaguely understands that this is a bad omen: "An owl seen the night of St. John's day / Means disaster can't be far away." Several weeks later, the bells toll for the tocsin, and a crowd rushes to the town hall. The poster announcing the mobilization has been put up. That evening, the women open the drawers containing their husbands' military papers. Following the joyous dancing, Gance then films a danse macabre in shadow play: small skeletons twisting in the wind and behind them, bells ringing, and crows with a dark, threatening air.

How to capture the emotion of couples saying goodbye at the fateful moment when they don't know whether their separation will last a few weeks—or forever? Gance concentrated on filming hands to express the dramatic intensity of these singular moments. The hands of a man carrying some home-made preserves for the trip; the hands of a woman furtively slipping a rosary into a mobilized man's pack. Two hands draw close to drink to a soldier's health, but the wife puts her glass back down, unable to drink. A woman lights a candle and joins her hands in prayer. Children's hands slip into an adult's rough hands—the hands of a father, no doubt. Timeless gestures of farewell, blessing, or affection, hands that embrace and then withdraw. All these gestures signify the emotional community binding the actors of this collective drama, as well as the insurmountable distance between men and women, between generations, between those who stay behind and those who leave for the front. The men's hands are rough, and they seem evasive in reaction to their loved ones' affection; the women's hands are powerless to hold the men back or soothe them.

Hands and tears both speak to the distress felt at the moment of farewell. Gance gives them an unforgettable expressiveness. A mobilized man tries in vain to console his fiancée. A canary sits in a cage, representing the loneliness of the woman left behind, and perhaps symbolizing fidelity as well. In the next shot, a man says farewell to his wife and two children. When he crosses the doorstep, the youngest child stretches out his arms despairingly as the mother bursts into sobs. The tears shed at departure are the very sign of the reality of war, which until then had been misunderstood or repressed. They testify to a harsh new reality: the familiar routines of family life together are over, and no one knows what lies ahead.

Unlike in silent film, where tears make it possible to speak emotions, photographs from this time show few tears at these otherwise quite dramatic moments. The only exception is a photo taken by Jacques Moreau, in which a man desperately holds his family tight, his eyes squeezed shut. He is unable to look his wife and son in the face. This is a rare, perhaps unique image in the immense corpus of photographs taken in Paris during the summer of 1914.[17] How do these outward manifestations of collective emotion shed light on the moral codes of France at war? Let us turn to the private life of the French at this point in time.

Tears also have a history—the history of emotions. They follow the rules of modesty; they mark the limits of what is permitted and what is not. During the course of the nineteenth century, tears in public were increasingly frowned upon. Only women's tears were considered acceptable, and then only if they were shed quietly, and preferably, in private. "At the train station [women] sob. They do have the right to do so, five minutes before the train is to leave," a reporter for *Le Matin* conceded. "They struggle; miraculously, their eyelids are barely red."[18] Many of those who were still children in the summer of 1914 connected their awareness of the reality of war—that is, the moment when *they*, children, entered into the war—with their parents' tears, a sight previously unknown to them. Simone de Beauvoir recalled: "I can see again the corridors of the Métro, and Maman walking beside me, her eyes brimming. . . . She had beautiful brown eyes and two tears were slowly rolling down her cheeks. I was very touched by the sight."[19]

However, as we have seen in photographs from this time, men and women instinctively took on the roles society envisaged for them: he, reassuring and protective; she, visibly upset, worried, but dignified. Moreover, it should be stressed how much the reporters and newspapers focused on the married couple, particularly those with children. This can be attributed to several reasons: the couple symbolizes stability in a society struck by war, and it symbolizes the unbreakable bond between the home front and the front lines. It also marks the culmination of a long process that recognized marriage as one of the fundamental institutions of the Third Republic, particularly marriage for love, so different from the unhappy unions found in nineteenth-century novels. The stereotypical figure of the summer of 1914 is well and truly that of a married couple soon to be separated by war. Yet married men with families barely numbered one out of three mobilized men.

Even more than the images of couples hastily photographed in front of train stations, the formal portraits of the mobilized men in their new uniforms seem devoid of any emotion. Many families had such photographs taken before the departure. During the early twentieth century, amateur photography remained faithful to the aristocratic codes of the formal artist's portrait. It was only at the end of the 1930s, and especially after the Second World War, that amateur photography began to show spontaneity. Sometimes, all the mobilized men in one family had their picture taken together: father and son, brothers or cousins, each wearing a serious and resolute look. The photographs were developed in two sizes. The photo card was designed to be slipped into a handbag or locket, like a kind of talisman, kept by wives, mothers, and sisters. Large portraits, more impressive, hung on the walls of bourgeois living rooms next to other family portraits, in a kind of genealogical continuity.

In the weeks that followed, the affectionate thoughts and prayers of loved ones turned toward these snapshots of the war's first days. Children were led toward the photograph as if toward a family altar. Since no one was granted leave until summer 1915, this was the only way for young children to remember a face that would inevitably fade with time. Destined to fight against forgetting, this photograph sometimes became an object of mourning. It was then taken out of its frame so that it could be bordered with a simple black crepe ribbon.

On Palm Sunday, a Catholic family would use a branch of blessed boxwood to decorate the portrait.

Over the long term, the war reinforced this regulation of emotions and feelings, the strict framing of time left to one's personal life, the primacy of the public over the subordinate and relative nature of the private. The leitmotif of societies at war is sacrifice: to be worthy of the soldiers at the front defending the country, to be worthy of the values they fight for, to be worthy of a nation invaded and threatened in its very survival. Faced with such high moral stakes, the ordinary heroism of the women and men who remained on the home front was celebrated as much as the heroism of those on the front lines.[20] And it began with the first hours of loneliness.

THE FIRST LETTERS FROM THE FRONT

Husbands and wives found themselves alone at night, often for the first time since their marriage. Families had been dispersed, and friends were separated from one another by an event that did not merely separate individuals but created apparently endless distance between them. "I do not speak of the isolation I find myself in when you are far from me; no matter how I look at our little girl and despite all the affection around me, I cannot get used to your absence, life with you is so sweet, life without you is unbearably heavy and hard," Marie-Josèphe Boussac confided to her husband in a letter sent less than a week after the mobilization. The day after his departure, she had only the strength to write this short message to him: "Only a note, my beloved darling, but a note of deep and tender love."[21]

The war rearranged relationships with stunning rapidity: between couples, parents and children, married women and their in-laws, siblings, and groups of friends. The departure of thousands of young adult men necessarily redistributed authority in the family, sometimes in favor of the wife but more often in favor of her father or father-in-law, or of any other man too old to be mobilized. With the separation, everyone became aware of the ties linking him or her to other people— ties that could have become obscured over time by daily life and habits, or the routine of marriage.

The distance between the mobilized men and their families also gave rise to a new "emotional regime": new fears and desires, or desires of a different intensity; new feelings, emergencies, priorities.[22] Personal correspondence offers unique insight into these changes. It allows us to identify how the war became part of private family life, and at what pace. In letters, the confession of sadness or missing someone coexists with chaste silence in regard to any suffering the writer is enduring; stock phrases can be found alongside more authentic expressions of emotion. "How can I explain to you, my dear, the feelings that have filled my heart during these last hours," Jules Portes wrote in a letter to his wife. "Some time will yet have to pass before I am able to collect myself and reflect." Several hours later, unable to bear it any longer, he sent another letter: "After the excitement of the day, I have a hard time warding off despair."[23]

The community of mobilized men was awash in contradictory feelings. But their wives, relatives, and friends could not stop talking about how the declaration of war had ripped their lives apart. They tried to cope as best they could via their letters. Families sometimes wrote to one another shortly after having said goodbye at the train station. Henri Barbusse wrote his first letter to his wife while in a train full of mobilized men; he had just spent his third night on the train.[24] One-third of the mobilized men were less than twenty-four years old; two-thirds, as we have seen, were still unmarried. The future novelist Louis-Ferdinand Céline, then known as Louis Destouches, was twenty years old; Charles de Gaulle was twenty-three. Both wrote long letters to their parents. On August 30, 1914, Roland Dorgelès began what was to be a regular correspondence with his mother during the war; with a touch of irony, he opened his letter with "Come on, don't cry, I haven't been killed."[25]

The soldiers did not yet have much to say about the war as such—only the lack of sleep and the uncomfortable nights on the train, getting to know fellow soldiers, and seeing new parts of the country. Some of them inevitably thought back to the moment of farewell, which was still fresh, and they described it at length, as if to capture every moment, as if to relive it. To live again, when the threat of death was already present, the expression on a face, a trace of perfume, a detail in a hairstyle. Physical absence is particularly manifest in these descriptions of last embraces with a loved one, sometimes in an almost palpable way. These are promises made for the future: "How I long to come back home to savor again those caresses you promised me and to forget, as you say, the rest of the world."[26] The newly mobilized men sought to construct an intimacy of words and emotions, as if to defy geographical distance and the dangers of war.

Few published collections of personal correspondence explicitly describe sexual frustration and physical desire. One exception is Guillaume Apollinaire's *Poèmes à Lou* and his *Lettres à Madeleine*, which were not published until after World War II (he died in the 1918 Spanish flu pandemic). Apollinaire feminizes and eroticizes the experience of war: "I am the white trench with the hollow white body / And I inhabit all this devastated land / Come with me young man into my sex that is my entire body / Come with me penetrate me make me delight in bloody voluptuousness."[27] For a long time, those passages thought to be too obscene were expurgated from published editions of Apollinaire's letters. More fundamentally, soldiers were little inclined to pour out their hearts and exchange confidences. The rules of modesty were even stricter for women; hence the words of a woman from Normandy named Yvonne Retour, in a letter to her husband Maurice, who had been mobilized in the summer of 1914: "I want you so much! . . . Sometimes, I'm ashamed of it."[28]

The Great War could sometimes break taboos and rewrite the rules of decency and modesty, but in a society constricted by morality, the control of oneself, one's body, and one's impulses remained the rule. Several months after the mobilization, the sociologist Robert Hertz wrote, "If I didn't say these things to you earlier, it's because in principle all our letters were read by the military censors, and not sealed, and it's unpleasant to speak almost publicly about private things—and because I well knew that you felt the way I did."[29]

Reassurance and protection were the key words of personal correspondence. Many men felt as if they were abandoning their families. Barely hours after their departure, they wrote home, their advice streaming from the front lines to the home front. Mobilized in the Territorial Army at age thirty-three, Hertz left to join his regiment in the army of the northeast by August 3. Because the Territorial Army was to protect barracks and train stations for the near future, he would not necessarily be on the front lines. As soon as he arrived at Verdun, he sent this letter to his wife back in Paris: "My dear, I'm doing very well. We had an excellent trip. I sat with Jacques-Ferdinand Dreyfus, who is in Verdun too, and other good friends. Our morale is excellent. . . . Don't worry—we only march on the 4th line—and will not be exposed. I tell myself all the time that we are happy and that the women are much more to be pitied. Provided that you can cope—take good care of yourself, take care of Antoine—don't get annoyed—don't listen to the news (all of it false) that's going around, don't worry about me (I'm writing this letter on my lap). I'm doing very well and taking care of myself. Have confidence—everything will be fine."[30]

CHAPTER FOUR

Trial by Fire

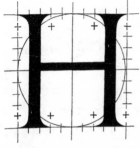UNDREDS of thousands of mobilized Frenchmen boarded their assigned trains and headed to the northern and northeastern fronts. What could they know of the horrors to come? On August 1, the men had only a vague idea of the situation. Of one thing they were sure: the war would be short, perhaps even swift. At most, they would be home by Christmas. Once on the train, there was no news from the outside world. Not even rumors. A military doctor from the 27th Artillery Regiment, Gaston Top, wrote in his diary: "We stretch out our legs while the endless train slowly but surely carries us to do our duty; none of us knows where exactly that is, except for the train's engineer. Each time we stop at a major station, someone brings him the sealed envelopes that control our destiny."[1]

The war got under way to the rhythm of trains. They ran at reduced speed, a little more than twelve miles per hour. Sometimes they stopped in the open countryside to let other convoys pass by. They halted in stations with unfamiliar names to take on rations and coal. Along their journey, the men were reassured by the locals' enthusiasm. They described it in their letters home (always the same obsession with protecting their families, making sure they didn't worry): a thick crowd gathered at every crossing and every station, bearing flags and flowers, shouting encouragement. Everyone had brought three days' worth of food. Some men had bottles of wine, cider, or brandy to be shared. It was hot. The trip seemed endless, and they passed the time by singing or playing cards.

More than five thousand convoys crisscrossed France during the first three weeks of August. They transported men to their assigned regiments, and then they took the regiments to their final destinations. This meant the war zone, for half of those mobilized in metropolitan France. For all the others, it meant depots, forts, and the protection of communication routes. The soldiers' routes defied logic. Lieutenant Jacques Rivière, whom we have already seen at Marmande, had left Paris for the southwest on August 4, instead of leaving Paris for the north or northeast. He would then head back to the capital with his regiment, before leaving again for the Étain sector, near Verdun.

Trains did not all converge on the northern half of France in a continuous back-and-forth circle. They ran between Paris and the provinces, between the interior and the war zone, and within each region. This doesn't include the soldiers who came from Corsica via boat, the thirty-eight thousand combatants sent from Tunisia and Algeria (such as Albert Camus's father), or those who came from the far corners of the French empire. "We leave for war as if for a pleasure cruise," as Henri Fauconnier put it when he boarded the *S.S. Syria*, bound for Marseille. To Fauconnier, the owner of a rubber plantation in Malaya, the European war seemed very far off: "One gets the feeling that a long sleep still separates us from it."[2]

In metropolitan France, the decisive period of August 5–18, known as the concentration (when the armies were arranged for the order of battle), required flawless organization. Never in all its military history had France called up such a large number of troops. A single corps, with two infantry divisions, or about forty thousand men, required eighty convoys. This was nearly ten times as many as the largest Paris train stations could handle. Detailed plans, organized hour by hour, contained arrangements for the transport of troops and matériel. The least delay in boarding and disembarking could leave thousands of soldiers stuck in a train station; delays at the other end could compromise the safety of the front lines. One hour was needed to board an infantry train, two hours for the cavalry, and three for the heavy artillery. To take a regional example, the Compagnie du Nord (Northern Railway Company) transported more than 889,000 soldiers, noncommissioned officers, and officers; 277,000 horses; and 70,800 guns from August 2 to the 5th, 1914.[3]

Once at their destination after several days of travel, the soldiers had to stay in a provisional billet before marching to the front lines. At the barracks, each had been issued his military uniform and equipment: a heavy, iron blue greatcoat, along with the famous red trousers introduced in 1829, turning the combatants into living targets. But who really worried about that? This was a time when the uniform's splendid colors were mainly meant to look majestic and impress the enemy. Cotton flannel shirts, hobnail boots with leather gaiters laced in front, a red kepi of the 1884 model, which since 1912 had been carefully hidden with a blue cover. The regimental number could be found on the front of the kepi and on the uniform's collar. The soldier's pack held a change of clothing, a bag with a day's rations, and various personal items. On top of the pack were a blanket and a tent canvas; on each side, another pair of shoes; and on the back, an entrenching tool, a canteen, and a cup. These made the soldiers even more visible than their red trousers when the sun glinted off them. And of course, each soldier carried the 1886 Lebel rifle, modified in 1893, with a bayonet, and he wore cartridge belts draped over him. All in all, each man wore more than sixty pounds of equipment, too heavy for the long marches of the early days of the war, too hot for the summer, and too visible in open terrain as well as in the forest.

Soldiers also wore identity disks around their necks. A strange talisman: on the front, last name, first and middle names, rank, and age; on the back, serial number and the name of the city where the regiment was quartered. During the war of 1870–71, the soldiers of the Imperial German army had received a similar document meant to help identify bodies. They called it the *Grabstein*, gravestone. Industrial warfare, with its massive body count, was about to begin.

THE BATTLE OF THE FRONTIERS

At the beginning of August, the French army of the First World War was still a nineteenth-century army. With their colorful uniforms and their idea that the war would be a succession of decisive actions, where moral strength prevailed over firepower, the soldiers very much resembled their ancestors of the Napoleonic era. The railways certainly played an essential role in the mobilization and concentration phases, but after disembarking, the infantrymen continued on foot, covering nearly twelve to twenty miles a day. Barely off the trains, regiments got under way at the regulation pace of two and a half miles per hour. Long columns of soldiers lined up in rows of four, rifles on their shoulders, bent under the weight of their packs and their equipment. After leaving Arras by train on the morning of August 5, Lieutenant Charles de Gaulle reached Hirson, about eighty miles away in Picardy, in the early afternoon. By the next day, his battalion had covered sixteen miles on foot to reach Maubert-Fontaine in the Ardennes, followed by yet another six miles to their camp: "The reservists who aren't used to this are suffering a great deal," he wrote. "The march is exhausting in good conditions. Arrived around 6 P M. The men didn't get soup until 10 P M. It was a tiring day."[4]

That summer, the heat was overpowering. Stationed near Sedan, the historian Christian Mallet complained about the "burning sun," the "perpetual whirlwind of dust," "clouds of flies and horseflies."[5] Uniforms stuck to the skin, feet bled in the new hobnail boots. A nail stuck in the sole, a badly laced gaiter—the pain could become unbearable. The recruits felt nothing but the sharp burning of blisters, the soreness of weary muscles, and the weight of their packs. As a soldier from Normandy in the 2nd Infantry Regiment put it, "The men cannot march anymore, especially the reservists, who are not in shape. The pack is too heavy, and the commandant has to threaten to shoot them in order to push them onward." Soldiers collapsed in the grass on the side of the road, too out of breath to speak. In his war diary, for the date of August 10, an army physician noted the name of the first victim from his regiment: a man named Malançon, from the 3rd Company, who died of heatstroke in the middle of the afternoon. He had succumbed to one of the great agonies of the beginning of the war: long marches under the beating sun, across the northern plain.[6]

The dust clouds raised by thousands of men marching toward the front lines could be seen miles away in the distance. The air seemed dried out, saturated with powdery white sand that covered the soldiers' faces, uniforms, and equipment. An infantry division on the march could stretch out over more than ten miles. After a few hours, the men advanced automatically, looking ahead, their only goal not to fall out of step. The infantrymen were at the head of the line, followed by cars carrying munitions, by mobile kitchen units, and then the cavalry regiments. In the early days of the mobilization, the French cavalry numbered 100,200 horses and 91,000 cavalrymen grouped in ten divisions, out of fifty-two active divisions overall; this gives a good idea of how important they were.

The cavalry conformed perfectly to the General Staff's idea of what the war would be like: a brief, rapid conflict determined by the element of surprise and the ability to react quickly. The cavalry also had a great deal of prestige. The French commanders had not given up on the heroic ideal of the cavalry charge, in spite of the reversals the cavalry had suffered during the Franco-Prussian War. Indeed, the use of lances had been reintroduced in the dragoons units in 1890. The 1912 French regulations concerning cavalry confirm its importance: "Only an attack on horseback with the use of blade weapons gives decisive and quick results, and it is the cavalry's principal mode of combat."[7] This valorization of the saber, the lance, and the sword was, moreover, characteristic of all European armies at this time. "From a military viewpoint, the negation of blade weapons means the negation of sacrifice and justifies the instinct of self-preservation," wrote the Russian general Mikhail Dragomirov, several years before the First World War. "It is, more simply put, the apotheosis of cowardice." Along these same lines, one of the most widely known British military theorists, Lieutenant Colonel G. F. R. Henderson, thought that the cavalry charge was "the most valiant act of war."[8]

In August 1914 the cavalry had to carry out surveillance of the borders, covering force missions during the concentration phase, and exploratory missions to prevent enemy incursions. In theory, it also had a combat mission. But it was badly armed and ill-protected against modern firepower, and therefore vulnerable. Hence the progressive disappearance of the cavalry from the battlefield, and the use of cavalrymen as infantry by spring 1915; it was painful to this elite corps to give up the elements of their prestige and join other units. "I don't want to live this passive life any more, a life to which the

entire army, infantry and cavalry, is condemned," wrote a former cavalryman. "I want to charge again, to go on reconnaissance again, I want to see the sun and the sky. . . . I've made
my decision, I'll become an ace pilot, in the light cavalry of
this war."⁹ In 1914, however, air forces were in their early stages. The French army had only about 160 planes at its disposal,
and they had difficulty reaching a speed of sixty miles per
hour and a maximum ceiling of ten thousand feet. Even then,
it took twenty-five minutes to an hour of flying time, depending on the type of plane, to reach that height. At the beginning of the conflict, the principal aerial role on the battlefield
was that of observation balloons, used to detect enemy movement and regulate artillery fire.¹⁰

The French and German armies were similar in size, but
used very differently. Of the 3,781,000 Frenchmen who had
been mobilized, only 1,700,000 were transported to the war
zone, while 700,000 were kept in reserve to compensate for
the losses of the first weeks. About 1,300,000 mobilized men
remained, and their roles and assignments were not clearly
defined. In fact, those in the French command did not believe
that their twenty-six reserve divisions could be used in the
same way as the active divisions. Moreover, they thought that
the Germans viewed their own reserves the same way. However, the German army's superiority on the Western Front
was due to its heavy use of reserve troops, which allowed for
a vast turning movement in Belgium and northern France
and for breaking the French defensive system.

At his headquarters, which had been established in a
school in Vitry-le-François (about halfway between Paris and
Nancy), General Joffre was convinced that the right flank of

the German army would stay south of the Sambre-Meuse Valley, and that it would not have the means to cross all of Belgium. Joffre, with his white moustache and impressive stature, led the war calmly, spoke little, and displayed a kind of bonhomie. The future Major General Sir Edward Spears, a junior liaison officer at the time, compared him to "any elderly bourgeois of the uninteresting little town of Vitry, whose habit it was to stroll of a summer evening before putting on his slippers and lighting his lamp." But Spears also observed: "His shoulders appeared strong enough and broad enough to bear any responsibility, as indeed they proved to be. His silence strengthened this impression of strength."[11]

Some eighty-seven divisions, of which fifty-two were active, had been divided among five armies arranged in an arc from the Oise to the Vosges. General Charles Lanrezac's 5th Army was in the Ardennes, and General Jean-François Sordet's cavalry corps was on the Meuse. At Verdun, General Pierre Ruffey commanded the 3rd Army. General de Castelnau's 2nd Army faced Nancy. In the Vosges, General Auguste Dubail headed the 1st Army. The 4th Army, led by General Fernand de Langle de Cary, was stationed a little behind the front, for lack of space. The goal was to attack the German army at its center, where it was thought to be the most fragile, in order to cut the front in two. The 5th French army was supported on its left flank by the British Expeditionary Force, which had begun disembarking at Boulogne on August 12, in order to take up position in the Maubeuge region.

The first ten days of August were relatively calm. Once they reached the front lines, the French soldiers received quick supplemental training, weapons, and rations. In a letter to his parents, Louis Destouches summed up the general feeling: "I think that the inaction won't last long, it's just a question of hours as to the great clash that will decide the fate of the war."[12] Billeted in a small village on the Meuse, the officer-cadet Lucien Laby had found a copy of *Les Misérables* in the house where he was staying. The noise of the enemy guns, firing nonstop, provided a counterpoint to his reading: "As it happens I'm at the Waterloo part of the novel. . . . This creates an odd effect. The men are cheerful; we sang all along the way. They have improvised a flag."[13]

The German armies were spread out all along the borders, from Düsseldorf to Mulhouse. Most of the troops were in the north, facing Belgium: the First, Second, and Third German armies, preceded by the First and Second cavalry corps led by von Richthofen and von der Marwitz. It was they who went on the offensive in Belgium and Luxembourg on August 4, with a considerable force of a million men. At the time, it was the largest invasion force in European history.[14] The Schlieffen Plan had made provisions for a rapid progression on the Western Front in order to envelop the French left flank and take Paris in about six weeks. The Germans would then turn toward the Eastern Front before the Russians had completed their mobilization. Time, the element of surprise, and the swiftness of execution were the determining factors.

Did the German plan have a chance of succeeding? Historians have frequently criticized its excessive ambition, lack of attention to operational details, humanitarian consequences (probable reprisals against civilians), and political cost. By proposing to invade Belgium, whose neutrality was guaranteed by the major European powers, the plan risked bringing

Great Britain into the war.[15] In addition, there was a significant difference between the plan as conceived by Schlieffen
and as followed by his successor, Helmuth von Moltke the
Younger (nephew and namesake of the leader of the Prussian
army during the Franco-Prussian War). Von Moltke decided
to send a greater number of troops against the Russian army,
which reduced the number of divisions on the Western Front.
This significantly weakened the right flank of the German
army in Belgium—in any event, more than the original
Schlieffen Plan envisioned.[16] Last, by mid-August 1914, the
first three German armies, led by von Kluck, von Bülow, and
von Hausen, met with unexpected resistance from the Belgian
army and *garde civique* at every step of the way.

The Germans' first obstacle was Liège, a major industrial
city blocking their access to the Meuse Valley on the south
and to the large central plain on the west. The city's fortifications, built in the late 1880s, were among the most modern
in Europe. A series of twelve independent forts built with
thick cement walls were spaced far enough apart from one
another to provide mutual covering fire. In front of each fort
lay thirty-foot-deep defensive ditches, as well as hastily dug
trenches meant to stave off any infiltration by enemy infantry.
A special force, comprising parts of the German First and
Second Army and led by General Otto von Emmich, was
assigned to take this seemingly impregnable position. According to the Schlieffen Plan, a single division would
have sufficed to capture Liège and Namur. In reality, eight
divisions were required to take Liège alone. The city fell
after twelve days of heavy fighting. Heavy artillery under
Ludendorff's command crushed the twelve forts one by one.

But what a price to pay! By the evening of August 17, German casualties rose to more than five thousand men.[17]

The German troops could then resume their westward march, preceded by two cavalry corps on reconnaissance missions. At one of the minister of war's visits to the French General Headquarters, General Berthelot remained confident: "The more we have the Germans on our left, the better it will be. For this will allow us to better strike the center." From August 18 to the 20th, the small Belgian army retreated in the direction of Antwerp. There, they launched three successive counterattacks against the flank of German troops, at the end of August. It was in vain. Brussels fell on August 20, Namur on the 23rd, and Antwerp on October 10. The Germans did not manage to reach the French border until the last week of August, which represented a significant delay compared with their initial plan. The logbooks on regimental movements document numerous cases of exhaustion, even the sudden deaths of soldiers unable to cope with the strain any longer. With twenty-five miles covered per day under the burning August sun, the Belgian campaign was agony.

In addition to the burnout from the forced marches, there was also the fear of francs-tireurs, whom the Germans imagined behind every window, in bell towers, and in the narrow streets of Louvain and Dinant.[18] A permanent state of anxiety heightened the feeling of exhaustion and reinforced hatred of the enemy. An NCO from a Württemberg regiment wrote, "Shots have been fired from several houses, which are then opened by banging on the doors with rifle butts, armed inhabitants are shot, houses burned. A seventeen-year-old was caught with a rifle in his hand and executed on the colonel's order. All the houses are burning, our men are doing a brutal job."[19] In the German soldiers' eyes, the franc-tireur was their exact opposite; lacking a distinctive uniform, he did not hesitate to attack at night or by surprise. "Our cavalry patrols, we hear, are being shot at in the villages again and again. Several poor fellows have already lost their lives. Disgraceful! An honest bullet in honest battle, yes—then one has shed one's blood for the Fatherland. But to be shot from ambush, from the window of a house, the gun-barrel hidden behind flower-pots, no, that is not a nice soldierly death."[20] At stake here was not only the outcome of a battle or military campaign but also the very idea of a "good death," one that honors the soldier ready to sacrifice his life.[21]

While the First and Second German armies executed a turning movement, the Third and Fourth armies went down the Sambre-Meuse Valley, crossing the Ardennes. On Germany's left flank, the Fifth, Sixth, and Seventh armies were assigned to push back the French invasion in the Moselle (annexed by the Germans after the Franco-Prussian War), meeting the enemy in the southern part of Meurthe-et-Moselle and in the Vosges. On the French side, Joffre was following Plan XVII to the letter, as it had been drawn up in 1911 and finalized in 1913: attack the enemy in the center, and then fall back to crush him on each side, as Napoléon had done at Austerlitz. As a matter of fact, this plan did not particularly suit the German plan of a turning movement in Belgium, since by counting on a central attack, the French emptied their left flank and essentially left the defense of the Franco-Belgian border to the small British Expeditionary Force. But who was worried? The cult of the offensive fed the illusion that the war would be over in a few weeks. The enemy's plans didn't matter much. As the *Instruction sur l'emploi des grandes unités* (Instructions on the use of large units, 1913) pointed out, "A vigorous offensive constitutes the best means of assuring safety."

The French attacked first, in Alsace. But their targets were more symbolic than strategic. General Bonneau's troops, based in Besançon, occupied Mulhouse by the evening of August 7, 1914. However, this area was not heavily defended by the enemy. Following the announcement of this victory, préfets' reports described "enthusiastic reactions" in the departments of Basses-Alpes, Puy-de-Dôme, and Deux-Sèvres, "deep joy" in Nice, and "great emotion" in Mende.[22] These bursts of enthusiasm were short-lived. The Germans counterattacked, retook Mulhouse on August 9, lost it again, and retook it on August 24. The French had to give up all of upper Alsace with the exception of the small city of Thann. This was Joffre's first failure.

On August 14, the 1st and 2nd French armies attacked the center of the German front in northern Lorraine. They won important victories during the early days of this offensive and were greeted as liberators in Château-Salins, Dieuze, and Sarrebourg. Joffre was presented with regimental colors that had been taken from the enemy.[23] However, by August 20, German forces were providing increasingly strong resistance after some initial retreats. They then managed to counterattack and push back General Ferdinand Foch, who led Castelnau's 20th Army Corps and had reached Morhange. The Battle of Lorraine was a resounding defeat and could have

turned into a disaster had the French not succeeded in holding on to their entrenched positions behind the Meurthe.

On August 21, the 3rd and 4th French armies, led by General Ruffey and General Langle de Cary, received the order to
march on Neufchâteau and Arlon, in southern Belgium. They
did not anticipate any resistance as they slowly moved into
the valleys surrounded by heavy forest. Sordet's cavalry, which
had inspected the area, had not detected any enemy presence,
nor had the reconnaissance plans. Aerial reconnaissance had
alerted the Fourth and Fifth German armies, led by the Duke
of Württemberg and the crown prince, to the French troop
movements, so the Germans went on the offensive. The
French suffered serious losses at Virton and Arlon. In Anloy,
civilians were often caught in the middle of the fighting, with
the Germans sometimes using them as human shields. Seventeen inhabitants of Neufchâteau, suspected of being francs-
tireurs working for the French, were executed on August 22.[24]
Farther to the south, the 3rd Colonial Division demonstrated
remarkable courage in a bayonet charge through the woods.
By the evening of August 22, three quarters of the division's
fifteen thousand men had been killed by German machine
guns.[25] Thousands of soldiers from the 4th Army lost their
lives before the village of Rossignol, a veritable epicenter of
this new violence, during the tragic day of August 22, 1914.[26]

In spite of the information he had received about the
breadth of the German invasion, General Joffre had long refused to acknowledge the risk of being enveloped by enemy
armies. By the third week of August, he had to accept reality.
He then ordered Lanrezac's 5th Army to draw near the British Expeditionary Force and head out toward the German

army. From August 21 to the 24th, extremely violent clashes—the most violent, in fact, of this initial period—took place between the Germans and the Allies, such as the Battle of Mons for the British and the Battle of Charleroi for the French.

Von Bülow was at the head of the German Second Army, and his vanguard initially clashed with Lanrezac's at the bridges over the Sambre. At first, there were scattered rifle shots, and patrols exchanged fire, soon followed by the whistling of shells. "A huge enemy shell ripped a horse open; the man leading him by the bridle was thrown fifteen or twenty feet, covered in blood from head to foot. We were frozen by the sight; everyone was flat on the ground, nose to the earth, in the dust, expecting to be killed from one moment to another."[27] Auvelais, Tamines, Arsimont—these small towns outside of Charleroi changed hands several times in the course of a few days, during some particularly murderous street fighting. In the chaos of battle, orders from headquarters did not always manage to reach the front. Both armies saw the Sambre as a symbolic border, and their obsession with conquering or reconquering its bridges prevailed over any larger strategy. Unlike the Germans, the French had field artillery rather than heavy artillery, which did not work well in the patchy fog enveloping the valley, along with the smoke from burning fires. As a result, they paid a cruel price. French infantrymen frequently had to run in front of enemy positions without any covering fire. Officers and NCOs had to improvise, and many fell while leading their men.

The scale of the death toll on the front from August 20 to the 23rd, 1914, is overwhelming. The historian Henry

Contamine puts it at forty thousand for the French army—twenty-seven thousand on August 22 alone. The number killed on this one day equals the total number of French soldiers lost during the Algerian War of Independence (1954–62). Largely forgotten in the French national memory, August 22, 1914, nonetheless remains "the bloodiest day" in French military history. German losses, for their part, were significantly lower. On August 23, British soldiers received the order to hold their positions at the Mons-Condé Canal, some twenty-five miles west of Charleroi, in order to stop the progression of the Germans' right flank. Among the British troops were veterans of the Boer War, who had learned how to hide in trenches and how to turn any structure into a fortress. They patiently waited for the enemy, who advanced in the marshy plain without suspecting danger. "We had no sooner left the edge of the wood than a volley of bullets whistled past our noses and cracked into the trees behind," recalled Walter Bloem, a German officer of the Twelfth Brandenburg Grenadiers. "Here we were, advancing as if on a parade ground. 'Huitt, huitt, srr, srr, srr!' about our ears, away in front a sharp, rapid hammering sound, then a pause, then more rapid hammering—machine guns."[28] In fact, Bloem was hearing the sound of Lee-Enfield repeating rifles and their fifteen rounds a minute, expertly handled by the British.

The men of von Kluck's army had failed to cross the canal, except in one place. Worn out, the British could not spend too much time rejoicing in their victory. On the evening of August 23, Field Marshal John French, the commander in chief of the British Expeditionary Force, heard the news of General Lanrezac's defeat at the Sambre and of his decision to beat a retreat the next day. Because the French did not hold their positions, the British were in turn forced to fall back. The Allied retreat began, with the German troops hard at their heels, hastening to take Paris and be done with it.

A NEW VIOLENCE

The Battle of the Frontiers is situated at the very juncture of nineteenth- and twentieth-century wars, at the moment when the modalities of combat took on a new kind of violence. The soldiers of the summer of 1914 found themselves under fire for the first time, in a new form of war. Yet their equipment, training, and collective mentality had left them unprepared. Faced with a storm of steel (to use the title of Ernst Jünger's memoir), the drill movements they had learned during their military service were no longer of any use. Even worse, their training hindered them, creating a gap between what they had learned and the way the technologies of combat had evolved.

For example, the men had learned to stay upright on the battlefield and suppress the instinct to hunch down or crouch when faced with shellfire. In barracks courtyards, they had endlessly repeated the same motions, shoulder to shoulder, responding instantly to orders shouted by their instructors. The soldier's "upright body" had become the symbol of military masculinity.[29] It demonstrated the ability to remain in control of oneself in any circumstances, and to remain impassive in the face of danger. The combat conditions of summer 1914 were a brutal retort to the ideas of the prewar period, and required a change in these "techniques of the body"

(Marcel Mauss)—a quick and disordered change, rather than anything actually organized by the French command.

The definition of battle was changing significantly as well.[30] Jacques Rivière, an acute observer of what he and his fellow soldiers of the 220th Infantry Regiment endured, described this change: "Battle does not in any way present itself as one might think. First, there is a lack of boundaries in time—its beginning and end are determined only afterward, by history—then a lack of boundaries in space, which means that although the positions of the two adversaries are clear overall, close up and in detail, the troops seem confused and muddled." Then he added, "Battle, before it starts and gets under way, is instead a state of being, a saturated compound of things, an urgent and confusing situation that gives rise to a thousand absurd and sudden confrontations, awkward encounters, to doubtful (I might say questioning) gallops and gunshots."[31]

In Belgium, the front had considerably expanded. By August, a line could be traced through Charleroi in the west, Namur in the center, and Dinant in the southeast. This was not a continuous line but a series of spots where clashes had taken place, spread out over several dozens of miles: the city of Namur, which resembled Liège in its modern fortifications and to which von Bülow lay siege; to the north of the Sambre, a country of slag heaps, factories, and metallurgy workshops, where soldiers could easily hide; to the south, fields of recently mown wheat, large brick farmhouses, and some woods; between the two banks of the Sambre, nearly sixty bridges of varying importance, which the French army hastened to fortify while waiting for the enemy.

In this densely populated environment, half agricultural and half industrial, modern warfare took place for the first time. With the huge disorder of deafening noises and the atrocious sight of mutilated bodies, a new kind of war was born. The confusion, disarray, and panic that it produced necessitated a tactical revolution, but this did not happen in August 1914.

Nineteenth-century weapons and uniforms coexisted on the same battlefield as industrial warfare. The weapons consisted of small-bore rifles with a weak useful range and efficiency. The French Lebel rifle, for example, used a magazine designed to hold eight cartridges, which had to be inserted one after the other—nearly impossible in the thick of battle. They were too heavy (nine pounds on average), and too cumbersome when equipped with their knife or needle bayonets. Yet the soldiers were attached to these weapons, which required a hunter's dexterity and savoir-faire. In their barracks courtyards, they had practiced bayonet attacks by plunging the blade in sandbags or mannequins. These exercises were meant to improve the flexibility and rapidity of execution, the implementation of attacks and parades, in a succession of movements and patterns borrowed from fencing. They valorized the personal aspect of combat, its courage and daring.

How different from actual combat conditions, where a soldier's ability during a charge mattered less than a kind of animal vitality, guided by survival instinct. "The body understands almost in the same instant that it sees," as the future novelist Maurice Genevoix put it.[32] With a rush of adrenaline, muscles contract and the energy released allows a soldier to run faster, in spite of the weight of his pack and rifle. Yet a feeling of confusion prevailed. In addition to the symptoms of stress—increased tension, accelerated heartbeat, visceral spasms—the men suffered powerful shocks to their sensory nervous system.

The smell of war was one such shock. Soldiers of centuries past were already familiar with it: the smell of dust clouds resulting from explosions, the smell of burned wood and gunpowder on the battlefield. The stink of corpses, mixed with the smell of dead and wounded horses. The sweetish, heady effluvia made the soldiers nauseous and left deep traces in their somatic memory. And then there was the sight of faces blackened with teeming flies, unimaginable for those who had only recently been civilians. These faces were nothing like those they were used to seeing at a wake. The reality and meaning of death had now changed. "Fortunately, fatigue prevents you from realizing all these horrors with great intensity, and we keep on marching with a kind of helmet on the brain," Louis Destouches wrote in a letter to his parents. "Nights never last more than two or three hours, the horses' backs are so badly abraded that the smell emanating from them is unbearable when the blankets are taken off."[33] In the evening, the soldiers smoked, and smoked some more, in order to dissipate some of the pervasive smell of death.

On August 22, the Germans set fire to the villages of Tamines, Auvelais, and Ham-sur-Sambre, which they had just conquered. The infantrymen choked in the acrid smoke of the fires drowning the Sambre Valley. Shells spread great waves of pebbles and earth that flew high into the sky before raining down. It was almost impossible to see the enemy lines beyond three hundred feet. Fellow soldiers—where were they? The

platoon leader's orders got lost in the noise. The men didn't
know where they were anymore. They fired straight ahead,
deafened by the surrounding noise. They reloaded their guns
as they had been trained to do, shouldering and firing without
really aiming, before taking a few steps and repeating the process. Some fell into shell holes, or took refuge in them, where
they spent long, even interminable minutes flattened on the
ground, not daring to make the slightest move. Trained for a
war like the Franco-Prussian War of 1870, they were caught in
the trap of industrial warfare.

The Germans had installed machine guns near the
bridges crossing the Sambre, as well as in bell towers (in
Roselies) and on slag heaps (in Ormont). These machine guns
confronted their assailants with an "invisible beam of countless minuscule metal ingots, each of which could kill."[34] A
hellish cadence of four hundred to six hundred rounds a minute on average meant that without artillery support, the
French infantrymen could not advance any farther. In their
accounts of the war, veterans used a variety of terms to describe the mechanical sound of the machine guns: the bullets
"whistled," "meowed," "roared." The men compared them to
"flights of hornets" buzzing above their heads. Those that
flew high in the sky cracked "like the lashing of a giant whip
of unbelievable brutality." In his war diaries, Lieutenant
Charles de Gaulle described his impressions of the moment
when his platoon took part in the defense of Dinant on
August 15: "I dashed forward, aware that our only chance of
succeeding was to act very quickly, before the enemy, whom
we could see flowing back, had a chance to turn around. I had
the feeling that there were two of me: one that runs like an

automaton and another who watches in anguish." He was then wounded by a bullet in the leg, which made him waver. "For half a minute, bullets rained down; it was horrifying. I heard them crack on the ground and the parapet of the bridge, in front of me, behind, beside! I also heard their dull thud as they hit the corpses and the bodies of the wounded lying on the ground. . . . With my leg completely numb and paralyzed, I backed off from my neighbors, corpses or almost corpses, and here I was, crawling in the street under this same endless hail, trailing my saber by its wrist strap, still on my wrist. How it was that I didn't end up as full of holes as a sieve will always be the biggest unanswered question of my life."[35]

In the Charleroi sector, thousands of infantrymen were cut down as they descended the hills leading to the river. "It had been said and repeated in myriad ways to the officers that on the condition that they attacked straightaway and without hesitation, they would in most cases find the enemy in the process of formation, that they would surprise them and easily win," General Lanrezac explained. "Now, as it happens, they found the Germans ready and waiting, with their infantry established on solid points d'appui, flanked by numerous machine guns."[36] Losses are difficult to estimate, but of the men that the French sent to battle on the morning of August 22, the number of dead and wounded may have reached 12,500 in Charleroi alone.[37] For the 25th Infantry Regiment from Cherbourg, which had fought near the village of Roselies, "in the evening, at the bivouac, a summary roll call showed that twenty officers and fourteen hundred men had been lost."[38]

In addition to the ceaseless dread of machine guns, there was the deafening noise of shells regularly falling on the battlefield. This was the great difference between the French and German armies during the Battle of the Frontiers: at Charleroi, the French 75mm field guns, supposedly better than the German field guns, had not been used to support offensive action. The French field artillery was prevented from doing its job owing to the lack of coordination between infantry and artillery, the fog at the bottom of the valley, and the limited visibility of the terrain, which was covered with factories, villages, and slag heaps. Conversely, the German heavy artillery sowed terror in the French ranks. The way in which the sound of the bombardments saturated the air led to panic attacks that were hard to control, as well as shaking, and difficulty breathing. Many soldiers flung themselves on the ground, arms around their head, and curled up in the fetal position, waiting in anguish for the next explosion.

In any event, most protection was powerless against shellfire. Soldiers took shelter in houses; the walls burst into pieces. The thickets scattered across the Sambre Valley were no good either. The future writer Pierre Drieu la Rochelle was twenty-one years old in 1914. He was wounded in the head by shrapnel in the battle of Charleroi. He testified: "Staggering, I reached the woods. I thought that the woods meant shelter. Shelter the way an ostrich puts its head in the sand, because steel fragments were refracted into thousands of fragments of wood, each explosion was multiplied into a thousand flights of green wood."[39] When infantry combat was under way in the forest, the dry crackling of tree trunks and branches gave the impression that shells and bullets were coming from everywhere. With these new sensory impressions, the Battle of the Frontiers gave rise to a new kind of fear.

DEATH'S NEW FACE

Until World War I, the reality of death in war seemed unchanging. Until the end of the nineteenth century, most soldiers succumbed to epidemics or to infected wounds, usually the result of blade weapons. But in August 1914, death had a different face. The conical, twisting bullets of small-bore rifles penetrated deeply into flesh, resulting in hemorrhages, fractures, or infections due to the presence of mud or fragments of tissue in the lesions. As for machine guns, soldiers had no chance against them due to their rapid rate of fire.[40] While fighting on the Côtes de Meuse, several miles from Verdun, Louis Destouches wrote, "Some of the riflemen want to attack the German batteries, but they have to fall back in the face of superior strength. And so as they retreat, they come across four German machine guns that cut two hundred of them down in two minutes, exactly seven hundred meters away from us. It was horrifying."[41] Then-Sergeant Marc Bloch, who fought his first battle near the Meuse with the 272nd Infantry Regiment, would long remember "the bees' song" of German bullets, inscribed "in [his] brainwaves as if they were the wax of a gramophone record," like "a refrain ready to go at the first turn of the handle."[42]

Most of the men hit by machine gun fire died at once. Officer-cadet Laby described them as frozen "in a running stance, their arms stretched out . . . like fallen toy soldiers."[43] Marc Bloch compared them to harvested ears of wheat.[44] The conflicts of the late nineteenth and early twentieth century, like the Boer War, the Russo-Japanese War, and the Balkan Wars, should have alerted military doctors to the devastating effects of modern weaponry. The future General Sir Ian Hamilton of Great Britain was one of many Western observers present during the Japanese attack on Port Arthur in November 1904, at the height of the Russo-Japanese War. He described at length the "bodies, or portions of bodies, flattened out and stamped into the surface of the earth" by shells, "rock splinters and fragments of shells cemented liberally with human flesh and blood."[45] No Western army drew any lessons from this experience, lessons for training conscripts, for sending men out onto the battlefield, or for dealing with the wounded.

Even worse, some physicians of the prewar period seemed to believe the myth of the "humanitarian bullet," one powerful enough to stop the enemy but without real danger to human life. It is astonishing to read the speech that the great Dr. Ferraton gave to the Paris Surgical Society in 1913: "With these [small-caliber] bullets, the pain remains small; the lesions are minimal enough for the wounded man to go to the first-aid station by himself."[46] The reality was quite different. Conditions on the battlefield made it impossible to deal quickly with the wounded and to give them adequate care. Men remained in no man's land for a long time, waiting for help. Except for a few instances, the previous custom of cease-fires for stretcher bearers to evacuate the wounded disappeared with the Great War.

Medical care on the front lines was provided mainly by inexperienced physicians, even medical students, while more experienced practitioners remained on the home front.[47] Chloroform and ether were used as anesthesia. Morphine, which had been discovered a century earlier, was still seen as a dangerous, addictive drug. Shell fragments caused two-thirds of the wounds inflicted; almost no one was prepared to handle this new kind of mutilation. Projectiles hitting the ground at high speed could cut a body in two or pulverize it. A simple shell fragment was enough to crush any part of the human body, cut off an arm or leg, or otherwise disfigure a man. The sight of the survivors was shocking. "Is it possible that a single bullet did this?" asked Maurice Genevoix.[48] He had just seen, advancing toward him, a cortege of what quickly became known as the *gueules cassées*, wounded men with severe facial injuries.

Because there were so many dead, military authorities initially had officers buried alone and regular soldiers together. These mass graves were dug hastily, for reasons of hygiene and to avoid the appalling sight of bodies abandoned on the battlefield. More often than not, shell holes covered with earth and quicklime were used for this purpose. Some of these collective burial sites have resurfaced recently, as highways have been built in the north of France, or during agricultural work. Archaeologists have observed that the bodies are frequently missing lower or upper limbs. This suggests that the soldiers were the victims of artillery fire, or that their bodies were ripped apart by a shell after their death. Some soldiers' legs have been found next to another body; the legs were all that remained. Weapons were removed and redistributed to other infantrymen.[49]

The very conditions of the beginning of the conflict—the war of movement, savage battles along the borders, then the French retreat before the German army—left no time to bury the dead. Battlefields themselves became mass graves. Indeed, many French soldiers were buried by the enemy, who did not take measures to facilitate later identification. Casualty estimates for these first weeks of combat remain somewhat vague. When the war began, the rule was that roll call would be taken every five days on average. Those absent were divided into three distinct categories. The first two consisted of those who had died in battle, and the wounded, who had been taken to the first aid station. The missing—buried under shells, carried off by enemy stretcher bearers or otherwise taken as prisoners of war, or deserters—formed the largest category. Their brothers in arms did not know what to write to the families, who anxiously wrote asking for news. The information collected in each company was integrated into battalion and regimental records, then into statistical records that detailed the number of French losses, month after month.[50]

By the end of August, losses were so huge that roll call was taken daily. Statistics recorded the number of dead and wounded by unit. Even if their precision is dubious, the various estimates carried out during the war and in the 1920s, as well as in demographic studies, leave no doubt: the first two months of the Great War were the deadliest ones for the French army. Nearly 235,000 men were killed or missing in August and September 1914—that is to say, roughly the same as the number of German casualties for the same period.[51] Seen from the perspective of how many soldiers were killed or wounded, then, the turning point of the war was not the beginning of trench warfare in autumn 1914. Neither was it the use of poison gas beginning in 1915, nor the massacres of Verdun and the Somme in 1916. In fact, the turning point came as early as summer 1914. At once, in just a few weeks, the collective catastrophe of the First World War engulfed France. The fabric of society had been ripped apart from the very beginning.

For officers and regular soldiers taught to believe they were superior to the enemy, these massive losses brought about a kind of collective shock: another major turning point. The Battle of the Frontiers left many families struggling with uncertainty over the fate of their loved ones. Shells had left many bodies difficult to identify. Others had been abandoned; there was no time to bury them, no time to mourn. Soldiers were forced to leave behind the bodies of their fellow men. Often, the dead were from the same part of France as the survivors, since regiments were still organized on a regional basis at this point in the war.

Yet another trauma had to be dealt with: retreat. When they left for the front in August 1914, the men thought they would stop the enemy at the borders, push the Germans back home, and advance until they gained a final victory in Berlin. No one imagined what would happen during the third week of August: the immense anguish of the defeat at the borders and the retreat in the direction of Paris. In his war memoirs, the writer and journalist Jean Galtier-Boissière remembered the words of a young girl he met in a village in the north of France: "Monsieur, you're not going to abandon us, are you? You'll defend us, won't you?"[52]

Many soldiers were in a state of moral abandonment. Some even pillaged the houses of French civilians who had fled just a few hours before. They also destroyed property, breaking windows and doors, turning over furniture. Since supply lines were functioning well in spite of everything, this behavior cannot be simply explained by lack of rations and equipment. Rather, it stemmed from the feelings of anger and bitterness that come with defeat.[53] Barely a few weeks after the war began, many French citizens understood—and many felt it in their flesh—that nothing would be the same anymore.

CHAPTER FIVE

The Shadow of Defeat

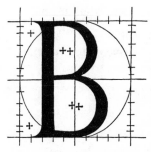y the third week of August, Joffre had seen his plans fall apart. He had thought that his army would be victorious and the battle short, but it all became a disaster. Never in France's military history had so many men been killed in so short a time—twenty-seven thousand French soldiers on August 22 alone, and forty thousand overall from August 20 to the 23rd. In his General Instructions no. 2, dated August 25, 1914, the chief of staff outlined a plan to regroup. It was necessary to "rebuild our left flank," he wrote, "by joining the 4th and 5th French armies, along with the British army and with new forces from the east, creating a mass of men capable of taking up the offensive while the other armies contain enemy efforts for as long as is needed."[1] This important document from the early days of the war is astonishing; it demonstrates an unshakable

confidence even in the very midst of defeat. Even so, a ninety-five-mile retreat all the way to Amiens signified a serious reversal of fortune. The illusion of a short war had been shattered; the general staff had lessons to learn.

EXPLAINING FAILED PLANS

Since the end of the First World War, military historians have interpreted the deadly Battle of the Frontiers in different ways. Some held Joffre alone responsible, thinking that since he doubted the extent to which Germany would invade Belgium, he delayed in providing sufficient forces to oppose it. Others stressed his sang-froid following the disaster of Charleroi, as well as his ability to organize the troops' retreat via forced marches and carry out a decisive counteroffensive on the Marne in early September.[2] Whatever the case may be, Plan XVII had been roundly defeated.

Yet everything had been carefully prepared. Of 3,781,000 mobilized Frenchmen, about half were concentrated on the borders. These were unprecedented numbers. Travelers arriving in Paris at the end of July were surprised to see thousands of wagons from different railway companies hooked up to one another, with inactive locomotives, waiting for the mobilization.[3] A simple white poster had sufficed to put this gigantic, collective enterprise in motion. Strangely, although Plan XVII had everything in place, it left the northern border entirely undefended, taking no account of the Schlieffen Plan—a plan known to the French general staff since 1906. Was this negligence? The reality was that Joffre had thought it necessary to first let the Germans advance into Belgium; then the French would attack the center of the enemy front.[4] "The swiftness of engagement will give us insurance against enemy maneuvers," in the words of Colonel Louis Loyzeau de Grandmaison, one of the leading strategists on the French general staff before the war. "What the enemy wants matters little. We have to know where he is and attack him for [our own] safety."[5]

Plan XVII could have been victorious, but only under two conditions. The French would essentially have had to concentrate their attack on a single objective, whereas Joffre had arranged his forces in such a way as to go on a double offensive in Lorraine, on the right, between the Vosges and the Moselle, and on the left, between Verdun and Metz. Consequently, his strategy was under threat. Moreover, he would have needed for the German center to be weakened while advancing across Luxembourg and Belgium, for it was there that the French had planned to attack. But Joffre had completely underestimated the strength of the Germans. In the French army, only regular soldiers were thought ready to go to battle, whereas the reserves were merely a supplemental force. Such was the meaning of the Three-Years Law. The Germans, for their part, had a completely different understanding of how to use reservists, whom they thought should be as effective as regular soldiers. No one on the French general staff had understood this, to the extent that on August 21, Joffre continued to estimate General von Kluck's First Army and General von Bülow's Second Army as totaling five or six army corps. In fact, they totaled twelve army corps, including five reserve corps. This estimate was therefore off by about 250,000 men! Joffre would later admit this mistake in his *Memoirs*, published during the interwar period.[6] In the aftermath of defeat, though, such a confession was clearly impossible.

Since his overall strategy could not be questioned for the time being, Joffre blamed the failures of the Battle of the Frontiers on tactics. At general headquarters, Colonel Alexandre lamented, "What can you do when the tool is bad and bends in your hand?" Considering all the errors senior officers made on the battlefield, he was not wrong. There was a lack of information on enemy forces and a lack of good liaisons between leaders and their units. There were absurd infantry attacks, made without artillery protection. The young Charles de Gaulle summed it up in a letter to his father: "Too often, the corps command, and especially the divisional and brigade levels, were behind the times, lacking great initiative, and insufficiently decisive."[7] Consider what happened at Charleroi. On August 23, around 4 PM, the 6th Infantry Division of the 3rd Army Corps ran into trouble dealing with German artillery fire. Deafening noise and whistling shells from an invisible enemy rang out everywhere. Faced with this physical and mental ordeal, the men had "fixed gazes, haggard and somewhat crazed."[8] At 4:30 PM, the general of the 3rd Corps was nowhere to be found. General Gabriel Rouquerol, who commanded the corps' artillery, had to take his place immediately.[9] General Sauret, apparently suffering from a fit of panicked terror, was not found until the next morning. He was in Barbençon, eighteen miles south of his general staff. This was an unusual situation, but at the time the French High Command saw it as a revealing example of a lack of leadership.

For General Joffre, there was only one solution: to get rid of all the incompetent field officers as quickly as possible. Of the four hundred French generals before the war started, a hundred lost their commands even before the battle of the Marne. Lanrezac, Poline, Ruffey, and Pouradier-Duteil were sanctioned. Castelnau, Maud'huy, Sarrail, and Franchet d'Espèrey were promoted, as well as a colonel who had distinguished himself in combat against the Saxons of the Third German Army: Philippe Pétain, now a brigadier general. When Joffre decided to demote Lanrezac, he wrote to the military governor of Paris, General Gallieni, "He [Lanrezac] was a remarkable professor [at the École de Guerre] who in wartime does not live up to the hopes placed in him. Do what you want with him." Nine army corps commanders, a cavalry corps commander, and thirty-three division commanders were also punished. They were sent into retirement, put on leaves of absence, or transferred to regiments far from the front—especially in the 12th Military Region, Limoges. Hence the French verb *limoger*, to summarily dismiss someone. These sanctions allowed the High Command get rid of incapable officers.

Such a turnover in army leadership was unprecedented, especially in a war that had just started. Neither the British Expeditionary Force nor the German army had to deal with such serious tensions. In his diary, Joffre referred to "serious command errors." The failure of the French generals was more than that—it was the sign of a cultural model in crisis.[10] Most of these men were, on average, sixty years old in 1914. They had graduated from the *École supérieure de guerre* (the prestigious French Army War College) between 1880 and 1890—in other words, at a time when the military used neither the telephone nor aviation. Steeped in nineteenth-century values, these generals treated the psychological effects of industrial warfare with contempt, either paying no attention to cases of shell shock or threatening to take care of them with firing squads.[11] Modern technology was also openly mocked. An engineer who graduated from a prestigious school and had been mobilized in the artillery installed a telephone switchboard in a command post; it was said that a general burst in and declared his opposition to the project: "My compliments, gentlemen, but this is hardly the moment for music!"[12] The battles of summer 1914 were thus conceived, directed, and led by men of the nineteenth century. This was also the case for the Germans, who shared the same reverence for the doctrine of the offensive.[13] The difference was that in mid-August they still had superior numbers and used their artillery more effectively.

While the failure of Plan XVII could have jeopardized his moral authority, Joffre remained perfectly in control of the situation. His command style stayed the same: imperturbable calm and unbreakable determination, which his enemies often described as despotic. The rumor spread that the *limogeages* had been planned a long time ago. Colonel Bel, of the general staff, allegedly had a notebook in which every general's name had the name of his replacement next to it in capital letters.[14] Knowing that he had the support of the government, Joffre did not worry much about these rumors. President Poincaré declared, "Numerous sanctions have been taken. Given the amount, perhaps some will turn out to be hasty or even unfair. But the essential thing is to make the strength of a superior authority felt everywhere, vigilant everywhere, and unbending everywhere."[15]

The search for scapegoats was not confined to unit commanders. Entire regiments disbanded under the deluge of fire, sometimes leaving behind weapons and equipment. On August 19, at Dieuze, in Lorraine, the soldiers of the 15th Corps suffered attacks by enemy artillery that the French 75mm field guns could not stop. The next day, on the heights of Morhange, General Foch's 20th Corps (comprising Lorrainers and Parisians) suffered heavy losses before retreating, taking the 15th and 16th Corps with it. The general retreat of Castelnau's 2nd Army happened next, followed by the retreat of Dubail's 1st Army, situated more toward the east. Although it was supposed to bring victory, the offensive in Lorraine ended in utter defeat.

Public opinion soon blamed the units from Provence in the 15th Corps: those from Antibes, Toulon, Aix, and Marseille. On August 24, Auguste Gervais, a senator for the Seine department, published a venomous article in the daily *Le Matin*, accusing these soldiers of "giving up before the enemy." In a telegram to the minister of war, Joffre in turn complained about those soldiers who "hadn't held up under fire and who are the reason our offensive failed,"[16] to which Messimy replied that the officers responsible should be identified and executed.[17] These rumors were unfounded, since the 15th Corps had merely followed the larger movement and had not provoked it. Nonetheless, the rumors aroused strong emotions. Not because they collectively targeted a unit, but because the 15th Corps comprised soldiers from the south, who were stigmatized as rebellious or too emotional.[18] Gervais mocked the "troops from lovely Provence," their lack of sang-froid, their "sudden panic." At once, deputies from the south went on the counterattack. How could the censors approve such an inflammatory piece? The minister of war was suspected of spreading the rumors himself and wanting to get back at the senator Georges Clemenceau by implicating his constituents from the Var, the Provençal department that he represented.

On August 26, Président du Conseil René Viviani thus summoned Messimy to dismiss him from the government. "Parliament is strongly against you," he said. "They reproach you for nominating Joffre as general in chief; they accuse you for the failure of the initial operations; they blame your brutality and your authority. . . . Didn't you say that in less than ten days, the Germans would be in Paris! Are you crazy?"[19] Negotiations at the Élysée Palace led to the formation of a new cabinet, still under Viviani's leadership, exemplifying the truce between various political parties: Delcassé at Foreign Affairs, Malvy at the Ministry of the Interior, and Ribot at Finance. Alexandre Millerand replaced Messimy as minister of war. Before leaving for the front as a reserve captain, Messimy appointed the energetic General Joseph Gallieni as military governor of Paris. Messimy went on to be wounded twice, once in 1915 and once in 1916. He ended his military career with the Croix de Guerre and the rank of brigadier general.

The Chamber of Deputies and the Senate had decided to adjourn their sessions until further notice, so the rest of the government was free to oversee the war. Contrary to the rules of the Third Republic, the two chambers had not been consulted about the cabinet reorganization.[20] The radical socialists were in charge of only three ministries, Interior, Labor, and Education, instead of six. The political upheaval stemmed more from the arrival of two Socialist ministers, sixty-eight-year-old Jules Guesde, minister at large, and Marcel Sembat, in charge of public works. On the other hand, this Union sacrée had no ministers from the Catholic right.

PARIS UNDER THREAT

Meanwhile, soldiers were fighting step by step to stop the invasion. Joffre had developed a defensive strategy that relied on forts and natural obstacles. He had ordered rail lines that might be used by the enemy to be destroyed. After considering a retreat via Maubeuge-Mézières-Verdun, he opted for Amiens-Reims-Verdun, some sixty miles more to the south. However, his plan had several weaknesses: the distance between the 4th and 5th armies, which Foch's detachment was supposed to cover, and above all, the lack of coordination with the British.

An important Allied meeting took place at Saint-Quentin on August 26. Generals Joffre, Berthelot, and Lanrezac met with the commander in chief of the British Expeditionary Force, Field Marshal French, and his chief of staff, General Murray. Joffre asked the British to lead counterattacks that would help him rebuild his forces in the Amiens area. French, for his part, was furious with Lanrezac, whom he accused of "abandoning the field" several days earlier and leaving him to face von Kluck's army alone. In addition to the personality clash, there was a language barrier. The French spoke English badly, and the British officers for the most part did not speak French. The army lacked translators at this time, which was a serious problem. How could the complex troop movements of various nationalities best be coordinated?[21] The failure of the Saint-Quentin meeting threatened the whole of the French High Command's counteroffensive.

Upon returning to his headquarters that evening, Joffre was informed of the defeat at Le Cateau, about twelve miles southeast of Cambrai. The British had lost no fewer than eight thousand men, about a fifth of their total troops. He decided at once to form a 6th Army, with forces from the Army of Alsace and the Army of Lorraine. He assigned command to General Maunoury, sixty-six, who had retired in 1912 but now returned to duty. Recently named military governor of Paris, Gallieni had barricades set up and trees cut down along the fortifications, in order to get a clear line of sight. Under the skylight of the Grand Palais, soldiers of the Territorial Army did weapons drills. At nighttime, the capital already looked like a city at war. Only the light projectors of the Eiffel Tower and at the city gates pierced the darkness. In the event of a siege, cattle had been installed on the racing fields at Longchamp and in the Bagatelle Gardens. It was 1870 all over again. In a week, 500,000 Parisians left the capital.[22] The cities of Senlis and Meaux also emptied out.

On August 29, General Lanrezac's troops carried out a successful counterattack at the Battle of Guise. The victory was short-lived, but it did surprise the enemy. The French rediscovered the use of artillery, which they had neglected since the war began. Even so, the men had been fighting for weeks and were on the brink of collapse. Joffre was struck by their appearance during an inspection: "Hollow eyes in gray faces, darkened by three days' stubble." Twenty days in the field seemed to have made them age by as many years. Joffre was still angry with the British. At the very moment when

Lanrezac was beginning his counterattack, Field Marshal French had given his men a "day of rest and refit." He then had them retreat too quickly, leaving the left flank of the 5th Army dangerously exposed. Moreover, French had let Joffre know that his troops were "worn out" and would not take up the offensive for ten days. After his victory at Guise, Lanrezac had to retreat in his turn. On August 30, the enemy crossed the Somme, upstream from Amiens.

Fortunately for the French army, the German troops were also exhausted by daily eighteen- to twenty-five-mile marches. Captain Walter Bloem of the 12th Brandenburg Grenadiers would later remember the "inflamed heels, soles, and toes of my wretched young lads, whole patches of skin rubbed off to the raw flesh."[23] The news from the east wasn't good for the Germans, either. The Russians had won victories in East Prussia—which Joffre had heard about via the French ambassador in Saint Petersburg. Von Moltke, who would transfer his headquarters from Koblenz to Luxembourg, raised two corps and sent them to fight on the Eastern Front. This was a fatal decision. They arrived too late to take part in the victory over the Russians at Tannenberg, and their departure no doubt weakened the German forces in France.

On the Western Front, superiority in numbers had changed sides. Remember that on August 2, of the 3,781,000 mobilized Frenchmen, only 1,700,000 had been sent to fight. The rest, made up of reservists and soldiers from the Territorial Army—too old to be put in the regular army—spent the beginning of the war in barracks or guarding railways. After the massive losses of late August, these men became part of the regular army. Two new armies were created: the

6th, commanded by Maunoury and assigned to protect Paris, and the 9th Army Detachment, led by Foch, at the center of the French front. This resulted in an Allied force of about a million men—even if the British could hardly be relied on just then—confronting a German army of 750,000 infantry.[24]

The French General Staff was not yet aware of this advantage. The only thing on their minds was the threat of a German advance on Paris, which raised the urgent question of whether the government should leave for the provinces. President Poincaré consistently opposed this idea; he said that he and his ministers would leave only if battle was at their doorstep. Viviani's cabinet was divided. Ribot and Sembat supported Poincaré; Doumergue thought that there was "more courage in confronting the blame of public opinion than in running the risk of being killed." The president of the Senate, Antonin Dubost, reminded everyone that the seat of government (i.e. Paris, since 1879) could not be moved without a parliamentary vote. It was finally agreed that a simple decree would settle the issue. This was illegal from the standpoint of constitutional law, but in these troubled times, the German threat prevailed over any other consideration.[25]

The situation was getting worse hour by hour. On August 30, enemy planes dropped several bombs on Paris, killing one person and wounding three on the quai de Valmy and the rue des Vinaigriers. Several days earlier, the Germans had burned Louvain and its famous library. Poincaré's diary sheds light on the fever gripping Paris: "More and more letters arrive. It's all criticisms, complaints, recriminations, and pleas from priests and women insistently asking me to dedicate France to the Sacred Heart of Jesus." A deputy for the Aisne reported that the German slogan was "Paris will pay for France." The Socialist ministers Guesde and Sembat wanted inhabitants to be armed in case of street fighting.[26] Poincaré and Millerand pointed out that this would expose Paris to terrible reprisals.

At 2 PM on September 2, the Germans entered Senlis, twenty-eight miles from Paris. At the Élysée Palace, it was immediately decided to find shelter for the Gobelins tapestries and the Sèvres porcelain. Similar concerns prevailed at the Louvre; the Venus de Milo and some seven hundred other masterpieces were evacuated by railway to Toulouse. All the administrative divisions of the government began packing up: the ministries, the Banque de France, the Monnaie de Paris, the *Journal officiel*. In the early evening, General Gallieni went to the Ministry of War. The courtyard was full of enormous moving vans and archives. The staircases were not lit. A doorkeeper took him to Alexandre Millerand, alone in his empty office. A proclamation to the people of Paris, signed by Gallieni, was to be displayed at dawn the next morning: "The members of the Government of the Republic have left Paris in order to give a new impetus to the national defense. My orders are to defend Paris against the invader. I will follow these orders to the very end."[27] At 10:30 PM, the president of the Republic and his wife quietly arrived at the Gare d'Auteuil in order to take the train to Bordeaux. Poincaré observed, "All the ministers are already on the platform, with their wives, their chiefs of staff, and civilian and military staff members. Everything gives the somber impression of an official exodus, without protocol but subject to military discipline."[28] By the next day, the *Berliner Tageblatt* was hailing a "German victory." The German press described Poincaré as a "vain, weak man thirsty for fame, who became president only with the help of nationalism, driven by chauvinistic instincts" and held him entirely responsible for the "French defeat."

But it was then that the German strategy crumbled in its turn. The Schlieffen Plan, it will be recalled, had arranged for enveloping Paris from the west, before encircling the French army. But prospects changed with the losses sustained during the Battle of the Frontiers, as well as the troops held back to control Belgium and those sent to fight the Russians. Lacking sufficient forces, the German High Command ordered von Kluck's First Army to change direction for the southeast. In so doing, it left its right flank open to the French. A breach of eighteen to twenty-five miles separated it from von Bülow's Second Army. The French High Command knew, thanks to aerial reconnaissance. They ordered an immediate counterattack.

On September 5, von Kluck received a message alerting him to the danger. The British Expeditionary Force and the left wing of the 5th French Army were advancing on him. Von Kluck's situation at this moment has often been compared to a man "stumbling while rapidly heading downhill and who has been ordered to regain his balance while gently slowing down."[29] The turning movement toward the west that he had to make in order to face the enemy was all the more difficult because nearly 160,000 German soldiers were involved. From September 6 to the 9th, fierce fighting broke out over a front of 185 miles, from Meaux (Maunoury and his 6th Army versus von Kluck) to Verdun (Sarrail and his 3rd Army versus the crown prince and his Fifth Army). What happened next is part of legend as well as history. Paris was saved in the nick of time when the "miraculous" Battle of the Marne was won, with credit going to either Joffre or Gallieni. Was the German defeat a consequence of the outsize ambitions of the Schlieffen Plan? Was it a stroke of strategic genius on the French side or a tactical error on the German side? One thing was certain: in France and Germany, the myth of a short war was over.

CHAPTER SIX

The Enemy Within

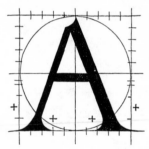 T the beginning of August 1914, hysterical fears about the "enemy within" emerged. With the outbreak of hostilities old anxieties resurfaced and intensified. Everyone, it seemed, was keeping French territory under surveillance. Soldiers of the Territorial Army, police officers, the *garde civique*, and ordinary citizens were at watch along roads and railways, at train stations, barracks, ports, and other strategic locations. A witch hunt was under way across the country for German spies and anyone aiding the enemy, referred to as *mauvais Français*, bad Frenchmen.

But what was a German? Official speeches and reports, along with news articles, leave no doubt. A German was principally a "Prussian"—the old enemy of 1870–71. The pillager, the vandal, the occupier in the Franco-Prussian War. The older generation had kept his memory alive and passed it on.[1] But a German was also a recently integrated person of German origin, anyone with a Germanic name, or anyone who could be stigmatized because of a slightly pronounced accent. This resulted in painful confusion for many from Alsace-Lorraine who had chosen France during or after the war of 1870–71. A German, finally, was the "Prussian" nearby or perhaps even at home. The struggle against informers for Germany turned into a struggle against German influence, and a break with anything and anyone that looked or sounded German.

The difficulty of clearly defining who or what was German only increased the perception that the enemy was everywhere, mixing with the French population. In his journal, Antoine Delécraz reported that a friend of his—claiming to cite a government minister—had estimated that there were 120,000 "undeclared" Germans in Paris. Obviously, no other sources confirm this number.[2] However, prefectural police archives record a large number of arrests of supposed German spies. Letters of denunciation were sent by the hundreds to neighborhood police stations, or directly to the préfet de police in Paris. In the provinces, daily prefectural reports sent to the minister of the interior reveal a similar trend, and not only in the regions close to the front. In the space of a few weeks, much like a diffuse and troubling rumor, spy mania gripped the entire country.[3]

"OF A VERY GERMAN TYPE"

From the earliest days of the war, strict legislation applied to the presence of foreigners on national soil. The law of *état de siège*, stage of siege, decreed by the government on August 2,

1914, described the entire country as a "besieged fortress" in a state of "imminent peril." The law markedly increased governmental powers in multiple areas, such as freedom of the press and freedom of assembly.[4] It also gave military authorities extraordinary powers to maintain order, even though the army ultimately remained subject to civil authority. This was not a military dictatorship.[5]

All foreigners, regardless of nationality—more than 1,160,000 people—were allowed to leave the country in the first twenty-four hours following the beginning of the mobilization. Afterward they would be registered and their movements limited. Sometimes they had to leave their homes and jobs, or to settle elsewhere in France. In theory, citizens of enemy nations were subject to the same restrictions as other foreign nationals. Their sole obligation was to evacuate areas situated within twenty miles of the northeastern and eastern borders, as well as the fortifications outside Paris and Lyon. Many thousands of Germans and Austro-Hungarians transited through Parisian train stations within a relatively short period of time. Some wanted to join their country's army, others to be closer to their families, and still others feared reprisals when hostilities openly broke out.

It was often impossible for them to find a seat in the trains leaving the capital. Returning in haste from his summer vacation in Brittany, the Hungarian novelist Aladár Kuncz went to the Gare de Lyon in order to leave for Switzerland. There he saw a crowd of civilians, laden with luggage, being held back from the platforms by armed soldiers; refugees were no longer being allowed to leave, as mobilized men had priority.[6] Germans who had somehow succeeded in boarding a train at the Gare du Nord in Paris were refused entry to Belgium by authorities there. They had to turn back, only to find themselves in Paris once again—where they were now considered enemies. On August 1 alone, three thousand civilians, including two hundred Germans and Austrians of military age, crossed the Spanish border at Hendaye.

On the second day of mobilization, the trap closed on all those who had stayed in France. They were forced to present themselves at police stations with their identity papers in order to obtain residence permits. Their movements were heavily regulated. They were prohibited from living in certain areas: twenty or so departments on the border, from the Nord to the Var, and from the Pyrénées-Orientales to the Hautes-Pyrénées for Germans and Austro-Hungarians, and a zone to the east of the Dunkerque-Belfort-Nice line for all other nationalities.[7] Each foreign national was completely dependent on the goodwill of local authorities. In Brittany, for example, the préfet of Morbihan refused to let "his" Germans and Austro-Hungarians leave.[8]

Families without residence permits were also arrested on the charge of "suspicion of espionage." "The police received five francs for each German without papers who was arrested in the street," stated a victim of one of these mass arrests, who was later detained in Brittany.[9] At the end of August, a young woman ended up in the police station of the 9th arrondissement in Paris. She had been walking in the square Montholon and asked someone for the time. Her strong accent attracted attention, and a small group formed. The police were called. They concluded: "She says she is Belgian but she has *cartes de visite:* Rosa Schuster, Frankfurt am Main."[10]

Bourgeois families who employed German domestics tried to hide the fact as best they could, even when vacationing at the seashore. But they could not prevent the denunciations of neighbors and other household employees. In large cities, the concierges who managed buildings were the most dangerous, since for more than half a century they had been a sort of unofficial neighborhood vice squad. This social regulation took on new importance with the mobilization, since some concierges now considered themselves responsible for nothing less than national security. On August 12, 1914, the concierge of 144 boulevard du Montparnasse went to her local police station to make a report. A certain Gustave Rissmann, married with two children and a lieutenant in the German artillery, had hastily departed her building ten days earlier, accompanied by his family. He took only one suitcase, and ordered that no one be allowed to enter his apartment. He had said that he would return to Paris shortly. This is what had alarmed the concierge, who feared he was a spy. A search carried out by a police inspector revealed nothing except a handful of letters written in German.[11] A landlady who rented furnished rooms near the boulevard Raspail worried about one of her lodgers; she said he was "of a very German type": "He told me that he had visited every port, Saint-Malo, Granville, etc. He locked himself in his room, wrote a letter, and went out. . . . He left (because of the Austrian mobilization) and paid only ten francs. I received a letter from Liège asking me to hold his correspondence for him."[12]

The Paris police recorded dozens of suicides. These were mainly men who feared being deported and forced to fight in the German army. On August 6, policemen from the Saint-Lambert police station were called in the middle of the night to the house of Jules Meisel, an Austrian sculptor married to a Frenchwoman. He had shot himself in the head rather than leave Paris and his loved ones.[13]

A final step in the regulation of foreigners came afterward, between the fifth and sixteenth days of the mobilization. The almost forty-five thousand Germans and Austro-Hungarians still living in Paris were regrouped in the Ivry and Saint-Lazare train stations and transported to prison camps in western and southwestern France. On August 5, the British government adopted a similar measure with its Alien Restriction Act, which culminated in the internment of thousands of Germans to the Isle of Man. French detention sites rarely resembled camps. In the southwest, in Bazas, detainees lived in the stands of a racecourse for several months, whereas in Périgueux, an abandoned garage sheltered about one hundred and fifty people, including the unfortunate Aladár Kuncz. He was later detained in Noirmoutier and then on the Île d'Yeu, until April 1919. Whatever the discomfort of their new living conditions, many welcomed their arrests with a sense of relief: "In the first days of the war, fights broke out in the streets of Paris; many German stores were destroyed and several Germans were beaten or injured. Some even died as a result. Finally, the police intervened and restored some semblance of order. . . . Here there is no danger; we are under guard and protected by the soldiers."[14]

A few escaped lynching thanks to the timely intervention of law enforcement. In Saint-Dizier, Haute-Marne, a German family of four found refuge at the police station. In less than half an hour, several thousand people had gathered in front of the building. The crowd shouted for the "Boches"—a slang term for Germans—to be turned over to them. The préfet ordered mounted police to disperse the rioters.[15] In Bagnères-de-Bigorre (Hautes-Pyrénées), violent protests broke out against German travelers attempting to reach the Spanish border, and against a dozen employees who had worked for several years in the local woolen fabrics factory.[16] Until then, foreign nationals had lived peacefully with their French neighbors; within only a few days they found themselves treated like enemies, forced to flee as quickly as possible, and often in dramatic circumstances.

Collective violence was more often aimed at those merely thought to be German or of German origin. Rumor played a decisive role in identifying the enemy; an individual could be branded a traitor rather quickly. If someone had a bad reputation before the war, this reputation stimulated collective violence against him and gave the violence a certain legitimacy. With the declaration of war, old quarrels between neighbors could now be renewed. Patriotic concerns magnified private disputes. On the façade of the city hall of Nogent-le-Rotrou in Eure-et-Loir, an anonymous poster called out: "Do you want to see a Boche? Go to 3 rue de la Fuye. You'll see a real one—her father was a Prussian. Her brothers are serving in the armies of Kaiser Bill—they may have killed or be about to kill your fathers, your sons, your brothers, your fiancés. I do not understand how you, the people of Nogent, endure her presence in your town, walking around like a real patriot, speaking only of her dear Emperor, of Greater Germany, which will emerge victorious and wipe out the dirty French. It's because I'm patriotic and wounded that I'm grumbling this way. If you share my opinion—act. Vive la France."[17]

Under these circumstances, those with origins in Alsace-Lorraine naturally risked being taken for the enemy. At the beginning of the war, a law was passed to help Gallicize family names with too Germanic a character. Alsatian volunteers in the French army were authorized to adopt their wives' last names or another name, with the idea that it would help them avoid reprisals if the Germans captured them.[18] But the greatest danger came from the French themselves. With this new patriotic fervor, anything that referred to German language or culture had become abhorrent. In the Paris metro, the station previously known as "Berlin" quickly became Liège. Rue de Berlin, situated between rue de Clichy and place de l'Europe, became rue de Liège. Avenue d'Allemagne became avenue Jean-Jaurès on August 19, two weeks after the Socialist leader's assassination. Groups of "patriots" tore down any plaques bearing the names of German writers or musicians. On menus in Parisian bars, *café viennois* became *café liégeois*, in homage to the city heroically defended by the Belgian army and awarded the Croix de la Légion d'Honneur on August 7.[19]

A new school year was approaching, and people wondered whether German should be taught in school. "When Germany once more becomes what it should have never ceased to be, an inoffensive mosaic of principalities, duchies, and free imperial cities, we will no longer need to teach German to French high school students," predicted *L'Action française*. "And when that time comes, we won't miss it. . . . [In the seventeenth and eighteenth centuries,] French culture reigned supreme in Western and Central Europe, and thus our language prevailed to the extent that other tongues were relegated to the rank of patois. France was safe then; in her schools, it was not necessary to teach the rude language and crude rhapsodies of barbarians."[20]

SPY CHASES

This wave of anti-German violence also originated with the fear of spies, fed by popular culture even before the war.[21] In 1906, William Le Queux's novel *The Invasion of 1910* met with great success. Initially published in the *Daily Mail*, it was sold by street vendors dressed in Prussian uniforms and spiked helmets.[22] In France, Arsène Lupin's adventures (*L'Aiguille creuse*, 1908–9; *813*, 1910), Léon Zazie's Zigomar stories, and the novels of Paul d'Ivoi and Paul Bertnay all propagated the stereotype of the masked stranger, identity thief, and soon-to-be traitor to his country. On the cover of the first volume (1911) of the *Fantômas* series by Marcel Allain and Pierre Souvestre, a menacing character in a tuxedo, wearing a mask and holding a bloody knife, looms large as he strides over Paris.

The vulnerability of the sleeping city suggested the vulnerability of the whole of French society, oblivious to the danger it faced. Spy denunciations aimed to mobilize citizens, make them aware of their responsibilities, and reinforce national cohesion in the face of external and internal danger. The spy literature of the 1910s follows a logic of unveiling, of bringing hidden truths into the public sphere.[23] It designates a threat and urges the population to stay on its guard. At the same time, it stigmatizes the liberal state as incompetent, unable to protect its own citizens. Paul Lanoir founded *syndicalisme jaune* in France; this was a union hostile to Socialists and to the use of strikes as a pressure tactic. In a 1908 publication, translated into English in 1910, Lanoir described at length the danger of German espionage and its necessary remedy: "As a preventive measure let us promote a formidable growth of hatred—hatred is always destructive—towards espionage in general and towards each hypothetical spy in particular. . . . The public must be shown these vile cowardly creatures who avail themselves of our all too hospitable laws and live amongst our all too confiding population; who establish connections and friendships amongst us, scatter Germany's thalers broadcast and ferret out our secrets. . . . Each one amongst us should look about him, in his own neighborhood and sphere of action, to detect any foreigner coming to plant himself therein. . . . From the day when spies 'at fixed posts' feel themselves to be narrowly watched, detected, and boycotted, and when every one refuses to have any relations with them, the *raison d'être* of the espionage service will have disappeared. None but wanderers and traitors will then remain to surprise our secrets and report them direct to the enemy."[24]

In the context of the war, this call to vigilance resonated with the population. For example, a forty-five-year-old man from Angers was photographing horses and military equipment as they were loaded into trains at the Gare d'Orsay in Paris. Thinking he was German, onlookers attacked him. In Brive, on the morning of August 3, a crowd assailed a Swiss citizen. His pursuers broke the window of the furniture store where he had sought refuge. The unfortunate man managed to escape through the roof. Anyone who had a wireless telegraph set, which had been forbidden following mobilization, was also suspected of espionage. Three sets were seized near the Porte Saint-Martin in Paris on August 13 alone.[25] In the resort town of Trouville, in Normandy, several hotels were searched for the same reason.

Suspicion was directed not only at real or presumed foreigners. In rural areas where people traveled very little, the war had brought in newcomers, which the locals found unsettling. Any new arrival soon became suspect: refugees arriving from departments in the north or the east, Parisian families fleeing the invasion, simple travelers whom the war had caught by surprise. It was the same story in Germany, where rumors flew that enemy secret agents—or Jewish spies, in other versions—were crisscrossing the countryside in cars filled with gold reserves. In France, the protection of railways, railway crossings, and bridges had been assigned to soldiers of the Territorial Army and to the *garde civique*. Full of disorganized energy, some worked zealously, systematically stopping cars they did not recognize. Identity checks could turn disastrous, as in Pont-sur-Sambre in the Nord department, where the victim was an unlucky customs officer: "I saw a uniform on the sidewalk. I shot. I did not know whom I was shooting."[26] In Ligny-Saint-Flochel, a gatekeeper killed a French lieutenant from Douai. On the night of August 4–5, two inhabitants of Toul, who had been transporting carrier pigeons to Commercy, were shot at because their car had not stopped at a checkpoint.[27] According to police reports, it seems that this kind of tragic mistake occurred all too often.

In his daily report to the minister of the interior, the préfet of the Saône-et-Loire complained about the rumors plaguing his department: "Last night, in the arrondissement of Charolles, the entire police force was called out to chase two drivers who had just sabotaged a railway. The investigation concluded that no sabotage had taken place. However, yesterday two arrests were made in Louhans, one of which appears quite serious. ... It concerns a certain Foret who should have joined his corps on the second day of mobilization and is therefore, at the very least, a draft dodger; he was carrying a piece of paper about the guarding of railways in Saint-Bonnet-en-Bresse."[28] Indeed, as a genre, the prefectural report had an important effect on the issue of German spies. The préfet did not just narrate events as they took place in his department. He dramatized the power he held in the name of the state and organized public priorities, distinguishing between false news reports and plausible or troubling news. The case of the draft dodger with a suspicious interest in the railway network is one such example.

To better understand this climate of suspicion, it is important to turn once more to sources that conceal neither the repetitive character of rumor nor its inherent confusion. For every event recorded in the large, lined notebooks kept by police stations there is a date, the civil status of witnesses, a general title, and a summary. The oral quality of speech is still clear in these records. The witness does not say, as the préfet might in his report: here is what I did to be in conformity with the mandate of the mobilization. He says: here is what I saw or heard and how I acted. In these registers, patriotic feeling is not confined to the margins; it is at the heart of the testimony, and it transforms small incidents into events. In the general chaos of the outbreak of war, many banal incidents take on a broader significance.

In mid-August 1914, suspicious objects were a recurring theme in police reports. They might be potential weapons, such as the "machine" discovered by a bookseller on the quai Malaquais in Paris on the morning of August 14. The municipal laboratory judged the machine "a certain danger, given its composition," without providing further detail.[29] Or they might simply be unusual objects that could enable the work of Germans or internal enemies. In such cases, witnesses point not to the danger posed by the object but rather to its presence in a time and a place where it should not be. The suspicious object is first and foremost an object that is unusual or out of place, whose precise meaning emerges only in the broader context of the mobilization.

The best example is the panic surrounding Kub brand bouillon cubes. This subsidiary of Maggi had displayed advertisements throughout France, featuring digits related to order numbers for registration services and to stamp duties paid to the state. Normally, these would have gone unnoticed. But in the summer of August 1914, this simple administrative detail took on a different meaning. The digits, which would be incomprehensible to the layman, became "mysterious." Their presence on advertising posters magnified their hidden meaning, and soon the layout of the billboards, their shape and their size, also became suspect. Delécraz, for example, somewhat recklessly forwarded the information that he had received from a member of the *Sûreté générale*, the national police: "It would appear that under each sign there were indications permitting provisions to be supplied to an invading army. In short, the Germans were to advance over our territory using the information collected ahead of time under these signs. They would have read France and calculated its resources like an open book."[30]

According to Alain Dewerpe, a specialist in French social history, this example illustrates a fundamental change in modern espionage. Spies would no longer limit themselves to transmitting confidential information at particular moments, as they did during the ancien régime. Instead, they would make the whole country visible to the enemy.[31] From this perspective, there is ultimately no better spy than the traitor or enemy within, who turns against his own country and knows its inner workings. Such was the xenophobic wave that befell Paris: "In every neighborhood, suspects were arrested en masse. A surprising and astonishing number of people took advantage of our hospitality while attempting to spy on us."[32] In hindsight, the accusations against the Kub bouillon company seem ridiculous. Innumerable spies and accomplices would have been needed to gather information about France's food supplies, compile this massive set of data, transcribe it in the form of codes on billboards, which could then have been spread across the French territory, all without attracting attention. But plausibility had little weight in the face of widespread suspicion. Beginning on August 10, the préfet of the Vendée had all Kub billboards removed; the préfet in the Haute-Saône also took down those for Continental tires. A few days later, the minister of the interior ordered that all signs along railways be destroyed. In less than a week there was a shift from diffuse rumors to private initiatives taken by certain préfets, to an order from the minister of the interior, and finally to spontaneous actions by citizens. In Périgueux in the southwest, in Bourges in the center, and in Perros-Guirec in Brittany, the crowd cheered on young men tearing down Kub advertisements.

SUSPICIOUS LIGHTS IN THE NIGHT

Unsurprisingly, suspicion became more pathological as the German danger neared. In mid-August, the préfet de police in Paris began to receive letters reporting large kites flying over the capital. In Lyon, a rumor circulated about a zeppelin coming over from Lake Constance; the military governor gave the order to shoot down the airship on sight. Citizens organized to defend themselves. The mayor of Lyon, Édouard Herriot, took part in the surveillance of the skies, accompanied by the director of the observatory.[33] Little by little, denunciations began to focus on lights in the night skies over large cities. A certain Troncsin, for example, sent a long letter to the Paris préfet de police concerning an illuminated advertisement for Cinzano vermouth, located on top of a building at the corner of rue du Havre and boulevard Haussmann. He claimed it was in the axis of the Sacré-Coeur Basilica and the wireless telegraph station at the Eiffel Tower. "I wanted to let you know," he explained, "especially because an advertisement for Cinzano, at this time, seems quite unnecessary."[34]

It had long been anticipated that a modern war would include aerial warfare.[35] In 1907 the first flights took place of Count Zeppelin's airships, which could stay in the air for almost eight hours and travel more than 225 miles. The British public was already concerned about German competition with regard to naval warfare; the development of the zeppelins, sponsored by Kaiser Wilhelm II, thus represented an

imminent threat. In *The War in the Air* (1908), the novelist
H. G. Wells had described the destruction of New York by
"flying machines." The French translation, published two
years later, was a resounding success. In the world of this invasion novel, no one would be safe from attack anymore,
since there were no more boundaries between the front lines
and the home front.[36] Combat would affect society as a whole:
civilians, women, and children, as well as soldiers.

In the field of international law, the conventions signed at
The Hague at the turn of the twentieth century offer a good
indication of how diplomats themselves had imagined future
wars. The risk of civilian populations being subjected to aerial
bombardment was discussed at length during the First Hague
Conference, convened at Russia's initiative in 1899. Articles 25
to 27 of the convention prohibited the bombardment of "open
cities"—that is, those that were not defended. They required
attacking forces to warn the population before any aerial attack, and forbade the targeting of hospitals, religious buildings, historic heritage sites, or museums (all of which were to
have been previously identified with red crosses or other distinctive signs). The terms of the convention nevertheless remained vague: how, exactly, were "open cities" to be defined?
Could certain buildings really be protected if explosives,
launched from balloons, often missed their targets?[37]

When a second conference met in 1907, technology had
evolved even further. Advanced military powers, such as Germany or France, were opposed to legal restrictions that would
put them at a disadvantage compared to less-well-armed nations. Moreover, Russia, which had convened the previous
conference, was now reluctant to discuss disarmament after

its painful defeat in the Russo-Japanese War (1904–5). The 1907 conference ended without significant progress. Certain internal contradictions can be seen between the restrictions imposed on naval forces and the general laws for warfare conducted on land. For example, bombing an "open city" was prohibited if the explosives were launched from a balloon, a zeppelin, or a plane, but allowed if they were launched from a ship, as long as the target was an arms depot or a factory manufacturing military equipment (Article 2 of the 1907 Naval Convention). Far from better protecting civilian populations from the danger of aerial attack, the vague character of these international conventions opened the door to large-scale bombardment.

In addition, improvements to aviation at the beginning of the Great War had made aerial bombing possible. As early as the summer of 1914, Germans organized raids on Paris and Brussels to sway public opinion. Meanwhile, Berlin stayed out of reach of Allied aviation. On Sunday, August 30, a German plane bombed the area around the Gare de l'Est. A woman was killed on rue des Vinaigriers following a gas explosion; four other people were wounded. Attacks continued until September 8, with a death toll of about twenty victims. A second wave hit Paris in the spring of 1915. But it was the bombardments in the spring of 1918, launched from long-range guns, which would be most deadly—notably the bombing of Saint-Gervais church during the Good Friday service. Several dozen women, children, and elderly people were killed.[38]

From the outset of the war, the press expressed indignation over these acts "contrary to humanity" and praised the courage of the civilian population.[39] Initially, Parisians' curiosity had taken precedence over their fear. The ghostly presence of fly-ing machines was part of the permanent spectacle of the mod-ern city; it excited the imagination.[40] In a silent and deserted capital, *flâneurs* observed the sky with curiosity. The darkness could be scrutinized for a German plane, which looked a bit like a pigeon—hence its name, Taube ("pigeon" in German). Some residents of Montmartre even rented their balconies to watchers.[41]

But excitement soon gave way to a nebulous anxiety, illustrated by the numerous letters of denunciation conserved in police archives. A simple glowing light in the night sky—a lit window, a publicity poster, a flash of light—was enough to indicate the destructive work of a German spy, an enemy within, or a *mauvais Français*. In the nineteenth century, the dark had been associated with crime, vice, social disorder, and conspiracy.[42] In an astonishing reversal of the collective atti-tude, light rather than darkness began to appear as a threat. In a letter addressed to the préfet de police in Paris, an engineer wondered, "In rue Le Peletier, there is a huge, twenty- or twenty-five-foot-high *red* arrow, pointing vertically in the direction of the Eiffel Tower. Who are the owners of the theater where this *special* sign is erected? How long have they been there? The sign holder at the cinema that existed before 'My Flirt' was German. Simple coincidence maybe? On the Grands Boulevards at 5 boulevard des Halles, the *en-tire house* stays lit up every night. It's a cinema whose owner is reputed to be a certain Monsieur Frankfort (?). These illumi-nations could serve as landmarks for foreign planes."[43] Two days later, the police chief in the Madeleine neighborhood also received mail concerning an illuminated hotel sign in

Place Saint-Lazare: "Without wanting to draw exaggerated conclusions, this Saturday during the day, while passing by, I saw two individuals whose shifty appearance attracted my attention entering this building (hôtel Bellevue). Now as I am about to mail this letter the sign, which has been alternately red and white over the last few weeks, has become for the first time (September 6) a fixed illuminated sign. I leave it to you to decide."[44]

In a conflict that required an entire nation to stand behind its soldiers, the home front constituted a source of military power. To win the war, it could not be weakened by disloyalty; civilians had to hold firm. Coming from ordinary citizens conscious of their duty but unable to interpret the significance of the information they were passing along, such letters effectively illustrate the spirit of self-mobilization that characterized the summer of 1914. Most of the time, accusations of spying and of sabotage targeted German agents directly. National, ideological, or religious minorities also functioned as scapegoats. The society at war could then project its own fears and frustrations on them.

ANTI-SEMITIC FANTASIES

A few years before the war, the nationalist press had taken up the theme of the enemy within, targeting recent immigrants from Germany and German Jews specifically. The daily paper *L'Action française* launched these attacks in 1911, on the occasion of the Agadir Crisis. The pamphleteer Léon Daudet revealed to his stunned readers the full extent of the plot that he claimed German agents had organized, on the pretext of investing in French industry. He published his account of the "German plot" in March 1913, with the troubling title *L'Avant-guerre* (Before the war). The first edition sold out its run of eleven thousand copies, and it was republished roughly fifty times between 1914 and 1918.[45] "We will show," Daudet wrote, "how, under the cloak of the republican regime, the German, guided by his intendant the Jew, whether his name is Weyl, Dreyfus, Ullmo or Jacques Grumbach, was able to find in France all of the facility, complicity and even betrayal that he needed to supplant our citizens in the various branches of commerce and industry affecting national defense; how he was able in this way to control our wheat, our iron, our gold, and to occupy, under the cloak of seemingly legal operations, the most important strategic points in the country, its nervous centers, its vital organs."[46] Daudet sought to present a tableau of all the sectors apparently held by German interests, from the large mills in Corbeil, directed by "the German Jew Lucien Baumann," to the chemical businesses in the region of Compiègne and the blast furnaces of Caen.

Though the author claims to be pursuing a methodical inquiry into German investments in France, this somewhat paranoid book also gives the image of a country under siege, sapped from the inside, eaten away by plots, and incapable of facing an attack from the outside. The figure of the spy was itself undergoing a transformation. In contrast to the external agent, sent by the Prussian army to France during the war of 1870–71, we find the blurrier and more threatening figure of the "sedentary spy," as Daudet called him—what we would call an infiltrated spy.[47] The goal of this new espionage would be to undermine national security from within. Arriving from a foreign country, the theory goes, the spy rapidly melts into the French population. He settles in a strategic location, practices a profession, and builds a family. After a few years, he takes steps to change his citizenship, and sometimes his name.

Daudet was particularly attentive to recent naturalizations. In his view, naturalization was a crude artifice that could not conceal the true nature of "German Jewish agents badly disguised as French citizens."[48] He therefore provided estimates of the annual number of naturalizations, which he claimed had jumped from 38,000 in 1896 to 120,000 in 1911. These numbers were completely imaginary and unfounded: a quarter of the 2,741 men naturalized in 1896, for example, were in fact married to French women, and half of them had been born in France.[49] The real target of Daudet and of some of his friends, such as the historian Jacques Bainville, was the new German law on citizenship, promulgated on July 22, 1913, and more precisely article 25-2: "Citizenship shall not be lost by any person who, prior to acquiring foreign citizenship, has received upon his application the written approval of the competent authority of his state of origin for retention of his citizenship." According to its author, Secretary of the Interior Clemens von Delbrück, "There are cases in which it might be in the interest of a German citizen finding himself in a foreign country to acquire, in addition to his old citizenship, a new citizenship . . . and to represent usefully the interests of his old country." The French minister of justice translated this in the following terms: "propaganda, espionage, voting, and, if necessary the use of arms."[50] After the outbreak of hostilities, French authorities worked ceaselessly to block these cases of double citizenship. They went so far as to proclaim the loss of citizenship for former nationals of enemy countries. All in all, 549 people lost their French citizenship during the Great War, in accordance with the laws of April 7, 1915, and June 18, 1917.[51]

But when Daudet published *L'Avant-guerre* in 1913, such radical measures were not yet in question. He limited himself to denouncing internal plots that facilitated the settling of German spies on French soil. For him, the person principally responsible for this "invasion" (Daudet created the neologism *espionenvahissement*, combining the French words for "spy" and "invasion") was Jacques Grumbach, the head of the Second Bureau charged with supervising foreigners at the Ministry of the Interior. Grumbach was a cousin by marriage of Mathieu Dreyfus, brother of Captain Alfred Dreyfus. "The first result of the affair of the traitor Dreyfus was a veritable invasion, the creation of an Anti-France at home," Daudet wrote.[52] The stateless Jew was the designated scapegoat; the far right press and, soon afterward, a segment of French public opinion would project their anxiety about treason and defeat onto him.

At the risk of being tried for defamation (which eventually did occur in the case of the Maggi dairy), Daudet listed alleged German spies and businesses. He drew a map of places controlled by the enemy: border regions, Parisian suburbs, large ports such as Caen, Cherbourg, and Toulon, and even the islands of Bréhat and Porquerolles. According to him, commercial entities, fortified sites, and coastal properties purchased by Germans were too numerous to count. On July 30, 1914, *L'Action française* published a long front-page article headlined "In Case of War: Against German Espionage," focusing specifically on food-related espionage. The principal target was Lucien Baumann, the owner of the large Corbeil Mills that fed Paris. The army was considering having the buildings occupied by colonial troops, but according to Daudet, once war was declared, it would be too late to ensure the security of the capital. "It takes no longer than precisely ten minutes to sabotage all of the machinery—the test was carried out at Baumann's command."

Rumors resurfaced a few days later via Delécraz. Many prominent Germans were said to have been executed, such as the director of the Astoria Hotel, who supposedly had a wireless telegraph set in his attic and weapons stockpiled in his cellar. The director of the Corbeil Mills was also named. Delécraz prudently observed in his war notebooks that it was more likely that Baumann had fled as soon as war was declared.[53] Other rumors mentioned large-scale massacres: the German embassy had been taken by storm, Ambassador von Schoen assassinated, and all of the Germans in Paris killed in the first hours of the mobilization. In fact, demonstrations against the German embassy boiled down to a few groups of "patriots" who came to shout under its windows on the evening of August 1. The police immediately dispersed them; von Schoen returned to Germany without any difficulties.

French opinion at the beginning of the war has often been portrayed as resolute and confident in a quick victory. This version neglects the great fear that seized the country: fear of enemy spies and of their accomplices, fear of a defeat on the home front rather than on the battlefields. The numerical and technological superiority of the German army was not what frightened the French the most; they were convinced that the army had learned the lessons of 1870 and had entered the war better trained than forty years earlier. Instead, public fear focused on enemy subterfuges and on the idea of enemy agents dispersed throughout France.

This fear was rooted in conspiracy theories, fueled by the still-vivid memory of the Dreyfus Affair, and revived once again in August 1914. The nationalist press did not hesitate to rekindle these anxieties, going so far as to describe Léon Daudet's articles on the German plot as prophetic. Fear took on myriad forms: fear of signs spread across the territory to guide or inform enemy armies, fear of spies and informers, fear of sabotage and of violent actions, fear of suspicious stories and defeatist remarks. In this decisive moment, civilians lived in the grip of rumors. As these rumors circulated, they spurred the French to vigilance and mobilization, awakening the ancient demons that are often reborn in moments of crisis.

CHAPTER SEVEN

Fears and Rumors

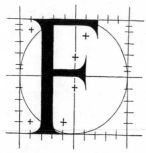 ALSE news reports! For four and a half years, everywhere, in every country, at the front as in the rear, we saw them being born and proliferating. They troubled minds, sometimes overstimulating them and sometimes sapping them of their courage. Their variety, their strangeness, and their strength still astonish anyone who can remember and does remember having believed them. The old German proverb is relevant: 'When war enters the land, then there are lies like sand.' "[1] Marc Bloch wrote these lines in a famous 1921 article on war rumors. They echo a large body of work, principally from the years 1914–18, produced by physicians, linguists, sociologists, and even simple observers.[2]

Rumors inevitably accompany the outbreak of war; they reanimate ancient fears inherited from previous conflicts. The fear of barbarian invasions and the violence they bring. The fear of enemy soldiers' brutality: rapes, mutilations, and atrocities inflicted on the wounded and the dead. The fear of graves, churches, hospitals, and historical monuments all desecrated. The visions of burning homes and refugees forced to flee. In the wake of the general mobilization, it took only a few hours for false news reports to spread throughout the country. As early as August 2, such reports announced the dynamiting of the Soissons Bridge, the presence of Senegalese soldiers on the outskirts of Paris, and the deaths of the famous aviators Roland Garros and Marcel Brindejonc des Moulinais; their aircraft had supposedly been sabotaged by German spies.[3] On August 3, several préfets reported a rumor that Joffre had died. On the 5th, it was said in Paris that uhlans—German light cavalry armed with long lances—had been seen in Saint-Cloud, in the western suburbs.[4] Contrary to stereotypes that identify rumor as a class-based and gendered phenomenon (rumor as the expression of the working class; rumor as women's discourse), the country as a whole was in the grip of this false information. The only difference between urban and rural spaces was in the manner and sites of dissemination: train stations, bars, the Grands Boulevards, and newspaper stands in the cities; markets, fairs, cafés, communal ovens and washing places in the countryside. The outbreak of war seemed to loosen people's tongues, especially in Paris. The novelist Georges Ohnet described "a kind of need to communicate with each other, to share news and to confide [our] worries."[5]

Rumor has both a timetable and a geography. By the second week of the war, border populations began to hear about atrocities committed by German soldiers in Belgium,

Luxembourg, and Meurthe-et-Moselle. The first mass execution of civilians occurred on August 5, the day after the invasion of Belgium. By the 8th, more than 850 civilians had already been killed.[6] The fall of Brussels on August 20, the massacres of Dinant on August 22–24, and the destruction of Louvain on August 25 inflamed the border regions, from the department of the Nord to the Vosges.

In Nancy, the préfet described the panic that took hold at the news of the Germans' approach. The city had been without news of the northern half of the department of Meurthe-et-Moselle since August 10, when it was captured by the enemy. The sous-préfet of the region of Briey was reported missing; the mayor of the small village of Éply near Nomény, subjected to several mock executions, had managed to escape. On the 21st, when a flood of refugees fleeing the invasion arrived, hospitals had become "a source of emotions irradiating the entire city." Saturday the 22nd, the préfet learned indirectly that the director of the postal service and his entire staff had left Nancy on a special train, without notifying him. News of this departure spread like wildfire. The mayor of the city went to the préfet to ask whether he too should leave; was it true that the train station would soon close? To reassure the population, which was beginning to flee, the préfet walked down the busiest streets of Nancy in uniform, accompanied by his wife.

On August 27, fear spread throughout the Lille area, and then Dunkerque.[7] In the small town of Annappes, the mayor, wearing his blue, white, and red sash, urged citizens to stay calm. Invoking the Hague Conventions, he reminded them that in wartime, humanitarian law protected civilians.[8] But the terrified inhabitants of the Nord department chose to flee instead. The sister of the deputy for the Pas-de-Calais noted in her journal: "They say that in Belgium, despicable German brutes have done such horrors to children that it is better to resign oneself to separation. In less than fifteen minutes, I threw together a suitcase for my children; they dressed precipitously; we ran to get passports and they left. Until when?"[9] On the same day, August 27, more than five thousand Belgian civilians arrived in Paris in the pouring rain. They told their stories in haste, as if getting rid of a bad dream. This frightened Parisians, who did not fully appreciate the gravity of the situation in the invaded regions. Some refugees were even arrested for disturbing public order. At the beginning, local authorities in the northeast of France had tried to turn the flood of refugees away from their cities, in the hope that their citizens would escape the "contamination of rumors." In a small village in the Ardennes, the mayor forbade the sale of bread to strangers. The préfet of the Aube had his refugees driven to the south of his department.[10]

The following testimony was taken at the police station of La Roquette in eastern Paris: "Alfred Lemasson, 21 years old, formerly a butcher, domiciled near Arlon (Belgium) states that the Germans (280 hussars, 40 cyclists, 8 uhlans) arrived in Jamoigne on August 16, forced him to march ahead of them as they crossed through the village, removed Belgian flags, broke the telegraph, set the priest's house on fire, and captured 21 prisoners. Constant, 29 years old, a native of Jamoigne, confirms these facts; adds that on the morning of the 11th, an officer of the French Hussars who had been wounded was killed by German soldiers, who opened his skull and removed his brain. He said that everything was plundered from the grocery store run by his wife."

In this assemblage of plausible details and manifest exaggerations, it is not difficult to recognize the apparent incoherence of trauma narratives, which bear witness to the intense devastation of the invasion. In these stories, the violation of bodies, torture, and mutilation are commonplace. Uhlans symbolize the enemy's barbarity. They are accused of charging at civilians, running them through with their lances, and cutting children's hands off with their sabers. Rumors, wrote Marc Bloch, feed on collective representations that predate their birth. "The uhlan is on every road, he knocks at every door, enters every city; he could find a way to pass through an arrow-slit," stated a woman who had lived through the war of 1870; "he possesses a cold audacity and acts with unparalleled cruelty."[11]

After spending a few days in Paris, Belgians and refugees from the department of the Nord proceeded toward the south and the west. Rumors tended to change as time passed, becoming less feverish and less active than during the first weeks of the exodus.[12] At the end of August, troubling news from the front replaced rumors of enemy atrocities against civilians. At the time, the French were fervently following the progress of the battles in which their soldiers were engaged. Photos taken in the summer of 1914 show crowds massed before maps posted outside city halls. But what did they really know of events in the combat zone? Official communiqués always arrived too late; the information they provided was too vague, and subject to military censorship. In the last week of August, public opinion felt doubt when the French army's withdrawal in

Alsace was announced, followed by the news of defeats at the Belgian border. Constrained by the strict regulations of the government-decreed state of siege, the press had kept the French in a sort of collective illusion. "Belgium holds firm; the invading army is seeing its offensive broken and is stopping," the daily newspaper *Le Matin* read on August 13, at the very moment when German heavy artillery was destroying Liège's forts one by one. "Many significant victories for the French troops," proclaimed the headline of *L'Écho de Paris*. "The butler could not imagine that the communiqués were not wonderful, and that the army was not close to Berlin," concluded Marcel Proust.[13]

We can thus imagine the shock the French felt on learning that their armies were withdrawing in the face of the invader. The wounded were sent to hospitals in the south of France; on August 28 alone, two hundred arrived in the city of Foix (Ariège). Met at the train station by a crowd of relatives and friends, they described savage acts they claimed to have witnessed on the battlefield. A captain of the 97th Infantry Regiment, evacuated to the department of the Ain, told the story of how Germans killed off the wounded and put out their eyes.[14] The préfet of the Tarn quickly had a poster put up in each village of his department, calling for people to remain calm.[15] The préfet of the Oise was worried as well; the passage of several trains of wounded soldiers through the stations of Compiègne and Creil had created panic.[16] Nothing is worse than the scarcity of news, he added; it is what feeds rumors. "The greatest relief we can bring to the public is the feeling that people are accurately informed," explained the préfet of the Corrèze. "The anxiety weighing on people because of mistrust would be infinitely more demoralizing than honest news about certain setbacks."[17]

One rumor persisted above all others: that of Belgian and French children brutalized, shot, or mutilated by the Germans. Recent studies have helped us better distinguish reality (such as the August 23 midafternoon execution of about fifteen children, in the neighborhood of Les Rivages in the city of Dinant) from fantasy or the collective imagination.[18] Indeed, beyond the violation of the Hague Conventions protecting noncombatants—which did not specifically mention the rights of children—the French perceived the deliberate assault on the weak and innocent as the most obvious manifestation of the enemy's inhumanity.

Any grist for the rumor mill could quickly be turned into traumatic news, following a standard pattern. On August 18, 1914, *Le Matin*'s front-page headline read: "Savages. They shot a seven-year old child. They deserve every retaliation." Citing a press release from a news agency, the newspaper reported that in the small village of Magny, a young boy who had been pointing at a German patrol with his wooden gun had been shot. The story, which has not been corroborated, was reprinted in the *Bulletin des armées de la République*. "The child with the wooden gun" soon became one of the symbols of innocence massacred by German barbarism. It appeared in a lengthy series of illustrated journals, on posters, and even in a puzzle for small children.[19] Théodore Botrel wrote a song about it: "The poor lad falls / He calls for

Maman / They bludgeon him with rifle butts / Glory to the German Kaiser."[20]

"The child with the wooden gun" was soon supplanted by a much more persistent and powerful myth: children whose hands had been cut off.[21] This rumor began to circulate at the end of August, first in the Netherlands, then in Great Britain and in France. It was said that among the Belgian refugees were children with severely mutilated forearms and hands. Or else another version of the same story: children's hands had been found in the pockets of wounded Germans or among the personal effects of war prisoners.[22] In this case, the rumor preceded the arrival of German troops in northern France. "There was talk of hiding children because the Boches arriving from Belgium were cutting off their hands, their arms," remembered a witness. "Immediately our parents hid us in the cellar, piling mattresses, duvets, pillows around us—we couldn't breathe."[23] Within a few weeks, the myth of "children with severed hands" gained significant traction. But it is very much a legend. No official document, among the many investigations carried out in 1914–15, confirms the story. Only the Bryce Report on German atrocities (May 1915) attempted to explain the mutilations, describing them as the result of rings being stolen or of saber thrusts by uhlans. But this report did not prove convincing.[24] The myth was more or less absent from the official French and British press; instead, it was representations of mutilated children in caricatures (Poulbot), postcards, and editorial cartoons (Willette, Hermann-Paul) that swayed public opinion.

In the fall of 1914, the rumor was still present, particularly in Paris. The writer André Gide volunteered at the

Franco-Belgian Home, a welcome center for Belgian refugees; he clearly believed the stories: "Mme Edwards, at the end of August (check the date) [*sic*], had told me of the arrival at rue Vaneau [Paris, 7th arrondissement] of a procession of children, all boys from the same village and all similarly amputated. . . . Cocteau came by after lunch without the photos, which he promised me for tomorrow evening; meanwhile, he led me to the clinic on rue de la Chaise, where we could speak with a Red Cross nurse who had taken care of these children. The lady was not there yet, and, expected at the Foyer, I had to leave Cocteau before learning anything. Ghéon also tells me that two amputated children, one fifteen and the other seventeen years old, [are] being cared for at Orsay right now. He is to bring me further information."[25]

These stories of young mutilated victims seem like a variation on the literary figure of the ogre. The German soldier, imagined as a devouring monster, dim-witted but guided by his instinct (smell) as ogres are, attacks victims who are smaller but also more cunning than he is: Belgian and French children. The "severed hands," however, never appeared in children's drawings from that time, even though these drawings abound with realistic representations of war violence. Historians suggest that this is an "adult myth, forged by adults for adults."[26] The "severed hands" rumor had several aims. It served to reinforce the instinct of the French to protect their children. It presented the war against Germany as a defensive war, defending the national territory as well as family and home. Like war rapes, violence against children is a direct attack on filiation.

Another rumor: German agents were suspected of traveling through France distributing poisoned candy to French children. Documented in many préfets' reports, this rumor is rich in meaning. Metaphorically, it points to the contamination of French society by enemy agents; this is the fantasy about German Jews advanced by Léon Daudet in *L'Action française*. But it also speaks to the vulnerability of French children, specifically targeted in a country where demographic decline had been one of the greatest collective fears since the end of the nineteenth century.[27] The stories related by the préfets of many departments in the south of France are reminiscent of fairy tales. In Lozère, travelers were said to have offered "sweets that looked like quince jelly, which caused poisonings."[28] An almost identical version featured the department of the Lot: in the small town of Gramat, a woman "wearing a blue dress drove through place de la République, throwing candies, many children had early symptoms of poisoning." In Corrèze, it was "a German man dressed as a woman"; in Figeac, seven individuals in dresses and wigs;[29] in Lavardac, near Agen, "a woman wearing a large feathered hat."[30] The prevalence of the theme of cross-dressing is not surprising in the context of the outbreak of total war, where barriers of gender, age differences, and the distinction between combatants and noncombatants were no longer respected.

The fear of children being poisoned was especially intense in Paris. Indeed, it was a question no longer of candy thrown to children from car windows but of a veritable conspiracy to poison the milk distributed by the Maggi company. As we have seen, a subsidiary of this corporation, the Kub bouillon company, had already been accused of helping the German army with billboards spread across the country. Police records for the 20th arrondissement in Paris show that as early as

August 2, 1914, rumor had it that two hundred children were fighting for their lives in the pediatric unit of the Tenon Hospital.[31] Delécraz confirmed the rumor the following day: "For the past two weeks, people have been saying that the Maggi dairies have been distributing poisoned milk to children . . . so that there would be no French people left after the war."[32] For the past two weeks: therefore, even before war was declared.

For several years, the company had been collecting fresh milk from a zone of a hundred miles around Paris. Pasteurized in factories and then transported in refrigerated trains, it was sold in eight hundred stores in the capital in 1914.[33] Each neighborhood had several Maggi stores, sometimes a few hundred yards apart. Historians have explained this campaign against the Franco-Swiss firm (suspected by Daudet of sheltering German spies) in several ways. Was it the climate specific to the outbreak of war, or was it simply rival businesses settling scores? Who circulated these malicious rumors? One thing is certain: the attack would not have reached such a high degree of violence without the symbolic force of the spy plot. Since the beginning of pasteurization in the 1890s, Nestlé and Maggi had built their reputation around preserving milk correctly and respecting hygienic guidelines. Nestlé had taken as its symbol a nest in which a mother bird fed her fledglings. Maggi claimed to combine respect for rural tradition with the modernity of new modes of transportation. In reaction to the "swill milk" scandal that had swept through large American cities in the 1850s, the two dairy companies proclaimed their ability to distribute a perfect food that could replace maternal milk. In early August 1914, the poisoned milk scandal was so great that almost every Maggi store was the target of looting in the days following mobilization.

VIOLENCE ON THE HOME FRONT

Around 11 AM on August 3, 1914, Corentin Pacos, a thirty-one-year-old servant, was arrested on rue Campagne-Première. In this shopping district near the Gare Montparnasse, in broad daylight, he had left in front of a Maggi shop "a death's head wearing a Prussian helmet and wrapped in a cloth stained with red spots." Taken to a police station, the Picardy native admitted the facts.[34] The window of the store was not broken; no merchandise was stolen; but the stained cloth associated the redness of blood with the whiteness of milk, the stain of crime with the putative purity of a mass-market food item. The spiked helmet called to mind the atrocities committed by the Prussian army during the war of 1870–71. On propaganda posters printed during the Great War, as well as in Abel Gance's film *J'accuse*, the helmet represents the brutality of the invading army. Classified by the police as a "public disturbance," the matter was therefore much more than a simple news story. It became the first in a long series of individual and collective actions. With the outbreak of war, conspiracy theorists who already imagined Maggi to be a German company felt emboldened to act. So, too, did a multitude of sometime rioters and looters. The exchange of rumors created a feeling of community, set in motion the designation of a scapegoat, and inspired the collective implementation of punitive action.

This means that we can trace the path of rumor and rioting, beginning with the neighborhood of Rochechouart.

Maggi's laboratory for the Paris region was located here. Then rue de Maubeuge, where other stores were destroyed. Buses had been requisitioned and there were fewer cars, so that the city was more silent and solemn than usual. Sounds of broken glass, mixed with shouts, resonated from one street to the next. From the top to the bottom of rue Montmartre, every Maggi shop was vandalized and looted.[35] On the Grands Boulevards, demonstrators attacked businesses with German names: the Klein leather goods shop, the Appenzedt Bohemian crystal store, the Salamander shoe store, the Pschorr and Müller brasseries. Violence then spread to the Left Bank and to the inner suburbs. Maggi stores were destroyed in Neuilly, Le Vésinet, and Chatou. In Melun, passersby destroyed a tram car simply because it bore a Maggi advertising poster.[36] Police records rarely specify the exact number of participants; most often there were a few dozen people, but also sometimes a few hundred and up to two thousand, as in Saint-Germain-en-Laye.[37]

In the provinces, targets included the Royal Hotel in Lille, a clockmaker's shop in Périgueux, and grocery stores in Bordeaux.[38] In Marseille, on the Canebière, a shop owned by a man with a German name was looted; the man was in fact a French citizen.[39] "This firm is French," read signs on the façades of some businesses. At a time when rumors blurred identities, it was essential to remind the public where one came from. In Paris, the boulevard des Capucines branch of the Peter-Cailler-Kohler chocolate company proclaimed that it was Swiss-French. The manager of the Hotel de Bade made it known that he was French, as did the manager at the Zimmer brasserie—but it was vandalized anyway. Yarff, a tailor on rue Montmartre, informed customers that he too was French, and that his real name was Fray (Yarff being an anagram). Some posted their voting or draft cards in their store windows; others put up photos showing them in uniform, sometimes wearing their medals from 1870.[40] "I hang my head in shame," wrote Gustave Hervé in his journal *La Guerre sociale*, "when I see our French businessmen reduced to putting patriotic bunting on their houses, nailing their military records on their storefronts, spreading on their windows a patriotism that smells like fear and terror, in order to shelter themselves from such acts of savagery."[41]

Shirkers got no better press than alleged German spies. Those business owners keeping their shops open adorned them with tricolor flags and rosettes. Then there were those who had been mobilized. They announced their departure for the front, so that the temporary closing of their shops would not be seen as running away. Some did it with a touch of humor: "Sleep in peace, the mattress-maker stands guard at the border." Others were more restrained: "Dolande, the owner, and his nine brothers are all serving their country." All promised their clients that they would return soon, in a few weeks at most. A shop owner on rue Turgot posted a small notice: "Verin, off to join the 3rd Dragoons, leaves his wife and five children in the care of the neighbors."[42]

Violence continued for another two weeks. On August 16, the dairy on rue Campagne-Première where a death's head had been left a few days earlier was pillaged. The assailants did not hesitate to dig up cobblestones and use them to smash windows.[43] According to the police, most were men who were too young to be drafted. They were masons, roofers, floor scrapers, waiters, bakers, deliverymen, market stall workers, and even young milkman from rival dairies.[44] All of them seemed to be overperforming their patriotic attachment. They acted out of a spirit of collective imitation, in solidarity with the troops or in a display of masculine pride. These groups of single men were sometimes joined by children or teenagers, whom the police called "Apaches." This late-nineteenth-century term designated youth gangs from the Parisian suburbs. The reality is in fact more disturbing. The violence of the summer of 1914 emerged not from the outskirts of the city or from marginalized groups but from the heart of the capital, and even from bourgeois neighborhoods that had traditionally been seen as quiet and safe. The aggressors often lived only a few streets away from the store that they had vandalized and looted. Their thefts were committed in broad daylight, in neighborhoods where everyone knew them, including the owners of the Maggi dairies.[45] Once the store was looted, the culprits calmly returned home. It was the objects of the looting that sometimes made it possible to confirm eyewitness testimony.

This outbreak of violence in Paris during the summer of 1914 still seems hard to understand. Its suddenness and brutality struck contemporaries. Even today, it seems to defy traditional explanations of how urban riots unfold. No neighborhood was really spared. The rioters had no particular sociological profile and few common traits. Their intentions were unclear; sometimes, they justified themselves by claiming to be attacking German shops; at other times, the attacks seemed to be driven by a need for financial gain.

Even if we cannot understand the rioters' exact motivations, the specificity of the outbreak of war appears distinctly. With astonishing speed, the enemy, real or more often presumed, was the target of collective hatred. Anti-German feeling took on a variety of forms: insults, attacks on property and people. After a few hours, a few days at most, the war's impact could be felt. Violence had exploded on the battlefield. Now it was everywhere.

CHAPTER EIGHT

The Sounds of War

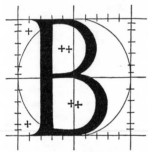 EHIND the lines, far from the front, rural areas now lacked the liveliness of a market day, the noise of voices in cafés, and the buzzing of workers in the fields. Gone were the sounds of the tasks that structured daily life. An uneasy calm remained in their wake. Women, men who were too old to be mobilized, and teenagers had done the harvesting at the beginning of August. Village life then began to slow down under the weight of the unrelenting summer heat and the anguish of waiting. The silence of war had taken over.

The very face of Paris had changed. There were fewer *flâneurs* in the streets and no tourists, despite the beautiful weather. Traffic had dried up because cars had been requisitioned for the war effort. One by one, theaters, music halls, and concert halls had closed. Everything that supplied the charm of the French capital—the constant effervescence of the boulevards, the city lights at night, and the impression of constant newness—had vanished. Joy was now suspect. "Avenue Trudaine is absolutely deserted," noted Antoine Delécraz in his journal entry for August 6. "The lugubrious silence that reigns over Paris, which we cannot get used to, is becoming more and more imposing."[1] This same heavy silence affected families. What little news there was of the war could be broached only with lowered voices when children were present; in any event, there was almost no news in the early days. In the absence of men, both the dinner table and the conjugal bed had become too large, as Jean Giono described it in his novel *Le Grand Troupeau*, translated as *To the Slaughterhouse*. In a few weeks, Haute-Provence was gradually emptied of its mobilized soldiers and horses: "So the mother took the son's place beside the wife. The mattress bore the son's imprint. The mother stretched out in the space the length of her son. And side by side, without saying a word, the two women listened to the unending noise of the herd in the night. Was the mountain planning to wither up the living beasts?"[2] Death had already insinuated itself into a country on the brink of war.

How did civilians cope with the ordeals of August 1914?

WAR HORSES: THE SACRIFICE
OF RURAL FRANCE

In the countryside, mobilized men left as early as August 2. The following week, village councils met at the request of préfets and took measures relative to the war: organizing local

agricultural activity, supplying provisions to civilian populations, and deploying the *garde civique*. Soon afterward, refugees arriving from Belgium and northern France had to be
housed. The first priority was to ensure the reaping and
threshing of the crops and the safety of future harvests.
About a quarter of the 5.2 million farmers in France on the
eve of the war had left during the summer of 1914. The re-
mainder gradually followed them as the war unfolded. Farms
were tended by men too weak, young, or old to leave for the
front, as well as by approximately 3.2 million women farmers,
already an active population in the countryside before the
outbreak of the conflict.

In the small and midsize family farms that made up most
of rural France at the time, men and women had long been
working together: the men in the fields or at the edge of the
forests, and the women at home, watching over children and
carrying out domestic duties, or in gardens and in barnyards,
tending to animals. These were distinct fields of activity, and
a man who had assumed the tasks ordinarily assigned to wom-
en would no longer have been considered a man. Some over-
lap was possible, however: if a woman "took up the plow" or
"went to the fields," it was "found to be natural": after all, "a
woman needed to do everything."[3]

We should therefore not overestimate the impact of the
war on the work of rural women. Before 1914, in poorer regions, it was not unusual for men to leave periodically to find
work in the city, or to participate in agricultural activities in
other regions. The beginning of the First World War changed
neither the participation of women in farmwork nor their
ability to manage family farms by themselves when necessary.

Viviani's famous speech to Frenchwomen on August 7, 1914, put at best a veneer of mobilizing rhetoric on their labor. "At this grave hour, there is no small labor. . . . Take action! Tomorrow there will be glory for everyone."

Women did not ask for glory. Rather, they needed resources for the harvesting, plowing, and sowing. After all, the army required extraordinary agricultural resources to feed millions of soldiers, but the male labor force had left for war.[4] Should the government call on foreign workers, men exempt from military service, men from the cities? Farmers on the Cotentin peninsula who employed sailors from the Cherbourg dockyard soon began to complain, because sailors knew nothing about agricultural work. Most of the time, villagers preferred to help one another out, rather than housing and feeding strangers. In the Tarn-et-Garonne in the southwest, the préfet was forced to send Italian workers to other departments because mayors refused to hire them.[5]

A sort of villagewide Union sacrée was forged across generations and families, suspending rivalries, at least for a few weeks. In Urville-Nacqueville, in Normandy, the mayor offered his combine for free to the families of mobilized men so that they could harvest their crops. In *Les Heures longues*, the writer Colette observed the return of those she called the "reenlisted of the earth"—a generation of elderly peasants "who, before the war, had been relegated to the fireside or to tending sheep by the harsh rural race" and who were now "waking up, coming back to life, guiding women, advising teenagers, replacing paternal authority," at the risk of rekindling tensions with their daughters-in-law or with the younger generation.[6]

Civilians also had to cope with life under military administration, which they saw as too nitpicky, making daily life even harder. The préfet of the Manche objected: "It is completely excessive," he wrote in one of his reports, "to require that our farmers carry a pass when circulating within their villages or the villages near their homes. They are having enough trouble bringing in their crops that such vexations, whose usefulness is not clear, should be spared them."[7] Travel, for that matter, was forbidden across France between 6 PM and 6 AM for all vehicles and even for pedestrians. Dawn could come as early as 4 AM, and night did not fall before 8 PM. At least five hours of work in the fields were being lost.

And how could threshers be used, when the army had already requisitioned the entirety of gasoline stocks? What could be done when so many millers had been drafted that mills were facing closure? On August 2, the préfet of Seine-et-Marne received more than two hundred telegrams from distraught mayors requesting deferments for their bakers.[8] In the southwest, flourmills in the Landes, Gers, and Basses-Pyrénées refused all orders for lack of personnel; flour stocks had visibly decreased. In the Hautes-Pyrénées, mayors had had to limit the amount of bread for each inhabitant.[9] In bringing about the mass departure of mobilized men, the war had nonetheless opened each village's horizon to include the country as a whole, and paradoxically caused village communities to withdraw in a kind of survival reflex.

In the collective imagination, war has always been associated with penury, sometimes famine. Quartermasters needed to feed millions of soldiers from one day to the next, and to feed them better than in peacetime. A man who ate an average of four ounces of meat a day now consumed from ten ounces to a pound or more daily, depending on whether he was serving in the regiments at the front or the rear. A standing army consumes bread in great quantities. For the French army, this was also true of wine, produced for the most part in the departments of Hérault, Aude, and Gard, and in Algeria. If there was a shortage of a basic necessity in the stores, the government risked having to deal with panic, vandalism, and looting. In this difficult economic context, the préfets' reports paid special attention to war profiteers. This issue would only grow more important over the course of the conflict. It was thus essential that the price of food remain stable, starting with the most basic and symbolic food, the source of so many fears and protests in the past: bread.

In an important overview of agriculture during the war, written in the 1920s for the Carnegie Endowment for International Peace, Michel Augé-Laribé summarized the obsession with running out of bread: the quality of bread "was modified, all sorts of substitutes were introduced into its composition, its consumption was limited, the sale of fancy breads was prohibited, and that of day-old bread ordered, [it was sold at a loss to the State,] but its price hardly altered. The minister of the interior was spared such anxieties as the specter of costly bread would have aroused."[10] The exportation of sugar beets had also been banned (September 30), as well as that of eggs (October 16), both fresh and dried fruit (October 26), and then charcoal and wool (November 23). There was a shortage of meat in the markets, because after the requisitions, vehicles were no longer available to take the animals to the cities.

Fish was in short supply, even on the coasts. War had deprived ports of their sailors and their ships. In Granville, in the Manche department, fisheries employed one of ten inhabitants in 1914. Most of the eight hundred sailors working in this sector had left in the first two weeks; the elderly had not been able to replace them. Cod fishing boats that had heard the news of war from their fishing grounds near Newfoundland had returned precipitously, although the fishing season was not due to end until November. As for the herring fishery, which kept many poor families in Normandy alive, it was hampered by the ban on night fishing.[11]

However, nothing worried people more than the requisition of horses. "What was strange during those days was that we weren't thinking or talking about the war much," a farmer remembered. "Everything came down to the horses, which had become almost the sole object of preoccupation for all of us. The state of siege that confined us to the village and the absence of newspapers forced us to concentrate on the present; and the present was the requisition of horses."[12] In France, between 490,000 and 510,000 horses were sent to the front from August 2 to the 4th, 1914, reaching a total of 742,000 by the end of December 1914.

Since the end of the nineteenth century, every December, owners of horses and mules had been required to make a declaration at city hall, concerning which of their animals were available to be requisitioned in case of war—something scarcely imaginable today.[13] Military authorities then assigned each animal to the branch of the armed services in which it would be most useful. These inventories were archived in city halls and recruitment offices in case of a general mobilization.

The military administration also set the prices that would be paid, on the basis of the animals' age and use. A draft horse for use by the troops was worth between 800 and 1,100 francs; a horse for an officer in the light cavalry would bring between 1,100 and 1,475 francs. The fastest horses, reserved for the elite cuirassier, could command 1,895 francs.[14]

On August 2, mobilized men and animals left a few hours apart. A teacher in Pallons, a small village in the Dauphiné, later remembered an impressive procession of horses: "They gathered behind the school. A scale had been installed on the path to weigh the amount of hay and oats necessary for each animal. The men appointed to carry out this task spoke in hushed, controlled tones. The same anxiety could be read on every face."[15] The procession set off toward the requisition center, followed by all the village residents.

Then came the crucial moment when animals that could be mobilized were sorted out from those who were too weak or old to leave for the front. Owners used their market-day savoir-faire to persuade the veterinarians on the requisition commissions not to take their animals, or else to buy them at a better price. The animals were presented first by village, then alphabetically by their owners' names. The horses' stomachs were palpated and their teeth examined. The commission could offer a higher price than that set by the price scale, but only if its members were unanimous. In order to avoid corruption, veterinarians had been forbidden to work near where they lived, in proximity to their usual clientele.[16]

Imagine the scene. The horses "arrive with their masters or their drivers; they feel themselves being touched, palpated by strangers, because they can differentiate men by their shape and their odor; they are separated from their guides, brought farther along, placed in a line along the sidewalk, near fellow creatures they do not know, then squeezed into various places, . . . all in an order that they do not choose, which necessarily gives rise both to spontaneous affinities and to individual antagonisms."[17] Separation anxiety increased the horses' nervousness, and they pulled on their ropes, whinnied at length, and kicked the ground with their hooves. The noise of these anxious animals contributed to the soundscape of the mobilization, much like locomotives or crowds cheering the departing regiments. Once they had been requisitioned, the horses had their hooves marked with their regiment number, were taken to the train station, and then loaded onto trains.

There was no open resistance to the requisitions in the summer of 1914, only a few attempts to escape them through subterfuge. Because brood mares had been excluded from the requisitions, to ensure the future of livestock farming, stud farms stayed full. Some farmers made "fake sales" to their neighbors who did not own horses, since the requisitions spared those who owned only one animal. A market gardener in the Loire Valley, for example, moved one of his horses to another town when inspectors passed through his village. He showed the commission another animal of similar color and size (which therefore corresponded to his official declaration), but which was seven years older. The fraud was later discovered and the man remanded to the courts.[18] To lose a horse, or sometimes many, was a catastrophe, especially when men were being mobilized.

The mobilization of oxen and dairy cows followed that of horses, and grievance letters soon piled up at the ministries of war and of agriculture. Mayors willingly recognized that the army needed their horses and bovines "to supply all of our brave men who are paying a blood tax," as one farmer put it.[19] But not to the point of jeopardizing the survival of farms. All in all, one out of every four horses was sent to the front in the summer and fall of 1914. It was a terrible shock, one now almost forgotten, for the half of the French population that lived in the countryside. Most of these animals died in the Battle of the Frontiers or the Battle of the Marne. In the absence of these horses and oxen, people were needed to replace them. A famous photograph from 1917 shows three women dragging a plow with all their strength. "There were no more plows to cross the land, to circle round the big plots of red earth," Giono wrote, describing the Provençal countryside in *To the Slaughterhouse*. "There were no more spades and no more hoes, no more picks and no more carts. . . . Only the sun remained, the rain, the wind, the earth. And they were free of men. The life of ancient times was starting once again."[20]

ALL QUIET IN PARIS

A Parisian returning to the capital soon after the mobilization would have experienced the same strange feeling as a farmer returning to his village after the harvests of 1914. Once the fever of the first days had subsided—when soldiers and their families flooded the boulevards and train stations—time seemed to pass more slowly. During the day, Paris had become almost silent. At night, despite the warm August weather, theaters and concert halls were empty. Since they feared gas shortages, municipal authorities had decided to light street lamps later and to turn them off earlier, plunging the streets into darkness for part of the night. As of September 1914, the fear of German zeppelins would entail more radical measures: streetlights were covered with lampshades painted blue; store displays and café terraces were no longer lit; residents were forced to install louvered shutters or curtains on their windows.[21]

Traffic and honking sounds had more or less dried up. A strange silence fell over the city. There were other changes; in the first week of August, pyramids of tires and gas cans began to pile up on the Champ-de-Mars, until they were several stories high. Requisitioned cars and buses covered the esplanade of the Invalides. Soon cars disappeared, much as horses had disappeared from rural areas—more than half of the vehicles inventoried in the Paris area on the eve of the war![22] No more *bateaux-mouches* or buses. The number of taxis shrank by two-thirds. There were only a few carriages, and they were pulled by horses too old to be requisitioned. The eight metro lines built before the war ran on a reduced schedule. About twenty stations closed as early as August 3: Temple, 4-Septembre, Europe, and Malesherbes on line 3; Saint-Michel, Saint-Sulpice, and Vavin on line 4; Oberkampf, Arsenal, and Saint-Marcel on line 5. To make up for the departure of men, it was necessary to hire the first ever women conductors and ticket inspectors. They took an accelerated one-week training course in lieu of the previously mandated three weeks. The woman ticket inspector, dressed in her black smock and shoulder bag, soon appeared in Paris metro stations; she would later come to symbolize women's wartime work.

Within a few days, Paris became an anemic city, a city without traffic. In his daily notes, the novelist Fernand Laudet compared the city's avenues to country roads, where the landscape was more open. "Paris is no longer Paris," he lamented, "it's like any other provincial city."[23] Echoing him, the anonymous author of *L'Âme de Paris* (The soul of Paris) rued the disappearance of the "Parisian spirit" in even its most important symbolic places, such as the jardins du Luxembourg. "Today, students and *grisettes* [young, independent Parisiennes] are nowhere to be found. One can walk through the garden to kill time, or wait at the corner of rue Soufflot for the newspaper vendors shouting 'La presse!' But no one lazes around there anymore. The spirit is elsewhere."[24]

Going to work, shopping, visiting friends: all of these daily activities took longer than usual, in addition to the endless lines in front of stores. Many windows bore the simple inscription: "Closed because of the mobilization." Others announced: "Reopening in September." Grocery stores had been mobbed as early as the first rumors of war. With its four million inhabitants—one tenth of the French population— the Paris region required considerable quantities of food supplies on a daily basis. A third of the residents of the Seine department would leave for the provinces during the first two weeks of August, fearing the German invasion, but the refugees streaming in from northern France and Belgium would soon replace them.

Paris, in contrast to London, had the advantage of being located in the heart of the richest grain-growing region in

France. The British capital depended on imports shipped up the Thames, especially from other parts of the British Empire; on the eve of the war, only twenty percent of the grains, forty percent of the dairy products, and sixty percent of the meat consumed were produced in the United Kingdom. In contrast, French agriculture was largely self-sufficient, even if the invasion of ten departments resulted in losses for the country amounting to a fifth of its grain production and more than half of its sugar beets.[25]

Three hundred thousand Parisians, or approximately one third of the capital's male workforce, had been mobilized in August. Among them were many young workmen, office employees, and managers of stores and businesses. The city had emptied itself of its lifeblood. "The only people we see are the elderly and the disabled," noted an observer. Among artisans and business owners, the activity rate fell by forty percent. Soup kitchens were opened for those who had lost their jobs and did not receive military benefits. A certain "moral economy of sacrifice" appeared: because they were shielded from danger and were not paying a "blood tax," unlike soldiers, civilians were asked to make generous charitable donations or carry out volunteer work.[26]

The mobilization of the owners and most qualified employees of many businesses had been enough to shut them down. In addition, the railways were closed to commercial traffic, and horses, automobiles, and trucks had been requisitioned. There were shortages of charcoal and other raw materials originating from invaded countries, such as Belgian wool, or German lamp glass and pharmaceutical products. Following the moratorium on bank deposits, businesses were also short on ready cash. France entered a period of industrial and commercial paralysis. But as the war was expected to be short, it was thought that these shutdowns would be temporary.

Businesses trying to cope with the "severe blow of the mobilization," in the words of Arthur Fontaine, a pioneer in labor legislation, soon had to adapt.[27] Department stores such as the Grands Magasins du Louvre, the Bon Marché, and the Belle Jardinière made bespoke uniforms and haversacks. Factories in the Paris region started making artillery shells, trucks, reconnaissance aircraft, and bombers. Renault factories, which had been operating in Billancourt since the end of the 1890s, were now building armored cars, light trucks, ambulances, gondolas for airships, aircraft engines, and munitions of all kinds: shells, shrapnel, and flares. In the capital's industrial belt, large factories were hastily built on former vacant lots, in Boulogne, Courbevoie, La Courneuve, and Ivry.[28] Hundreds of small workshops were also called on to build spare parts and to meet the army's most pressing needs.

Soon, the war also allowed an increasingly nitpicking bureaucracy to prosper, in one of the many manifestations of what the historian Pierre Renouvin later called "the invasion of government control" or *étatisme*. This meant an abundance of new paperwork, such as attestations, certificates, food vouchers, which people could obtain only after interminable waits at city halls and other public buildings. "No one complains; the people's submission and approbation is unanimous," wrote Fernand Laudet. "At this moment, it is clear that there are a thousand ways of showing one's patriotism, and none must be neglected."[29]

A COUNTRY UNDER CONTROL

The absence of news from the front distressed Parisians the most. On August 5, two days after the declaration of war, Delécraz observed people gathering in front of the book-stores in his neighborhood; large maps of the northern and northeastern borders had been posted in the windows. Every day, it was announced that the locations of the regiments would be added, but there were constant delays. Looking for some kind of mutual support, people continued to assemble in front of the maps to look for the names of towns where the trains of mobilized men had headed. In the absence of any specific information, people shared the latest rumors about the German invasion, spread by the refugees who had begun to pour in. "Where are the wounded? Who are the dead? We were told to go to the barracks at Penthemont, where we filled out a form whose stub we were told to keep," Laudet remembered. "We then had a week to present this piece of paper, a kind of receipt for our anguish, at city hall, where we would receive one of the three following responses: "Soldier X is not on the list of the killed or the wounded . . . Soldier X is wounded . . . Soldier X was killed in action."[30]

The state of siege decreed on August 2 completely trans-formed daily life. Meetings could be outlawed; the homes of private citizens could be searched and their occupants evict-ed. In 1870–71, only about forty departments had been subject to such regulations. From August 3 onward, the entry points to the capital were closed between 6 PM and 6 AM. During the day, a pass was required to leave and enter Paris. The préfet de police himself stressed the absurdity of the situation:

there were unemployed workers looking for jobs in the suburbs. To get there, they needed to ride their bicycles, but they were refused passes on the grounds that they could not produce certificates attesting that they had confirmed employment![31] Little by little, these checks were loosened. In many places, however, those traveling by tram still had to get off fifty yards from the city, go through the fortifications on foot, and then get on another tram in order to continue their journey.[32]

Some of the more officious mayors of Paris suburbs had roadblocks installed to bar entry to their villages after dusk. Paradoxically, although we may think of France in the summer of 1914 as united by the general mobilization, it was also a fragmented country. Multiple checkpoints impeded circulation from one city to the next. Within a few weeks, all public spaces would fall under the supervision of the army. From August 2 onward, public gatherings were, in theory, forbidden. On August 4, new rules mandated that cafés close at 8 PM and restaurants at 9:30 PM. Starting on August 14, all adults were required to carry their identity papers. For men, this also meant their military certificates; draft dodgers, though few, were being hunted down. On August 17, the sale of absinthe was forbidden in bars. What a contrast with the festive patriotism of tricolor bunting on public buildings! The stiffening of regulations gave Paris a serious and sad look. The Opéra-Comique's season premiere, which typically marked the reopening of Paris theaters, would not come until December.

A kind of "moral crusade" was unleashed in 1914: the ban on absinthe, the fight against alcoholism and prostitution, the

denunciation of adulterous wives, the regulation of the opening hours of theaters and cabarets.[33] Those who supported
these measures were members of the government or of Catholic "vigilance associations." Mobilization was a golden op-
portunity to reconfigure life in the capital, explained the
anonymous author of *L'Âme de Paris*. Before the war, "Paris
had become only cinemas and boxing matches; women walked
around half-naked in our streets. . . . One could no longer eat
roast beef or drink coffee without being assailed by fiddlers
from Batignolles wearing Hungarian costume. Paris, like a
tired old clown, didn't know what to come up with next in
order to keep its title as entertainer of the four corners of the
world! And now a poster glued to the wall had swept all that
away; and, like a storm wind that blows away everything it
encounters, this wind passed, removing the clowns' false noses and face paint."[34]

In the end, it was a question more of supervising French
society than of regenerating it. The other belligerent powers
experienced similar evolutions. Germany limited the consumption of alcohol. Great Britain moved up pub closing
hours, and considered canceling the national soccer champi-
onship as early as fall 1914. Working-class leisure activities
were viewed with suspicion, as fostering idleness or as distrac-
tions that took workers away from the war effort. The gravity
of the moment certainly required restraint. In the illustrated
newspaper *Excelsior*, an editorial writer invited Parisian wom-
en to don the more austere dress appropriate to the circumstances: "There is something a bit shocking, when our hearts
are full of sadness and anxiety, in seeing women wearing
fashions that are too '*modern style*' or too outlandish, with

corsages that are too flowery."[35] The call was repeated a month later by the Catholic daily *La Croix*, in a tone appropriate to its readership: "At a time when our soldiers are shedding their blood for their country, when the people of France are on their knees pleading for salvation, we believe that we must call on Christian women to react against outlandish or indecent outfits, fashions that have been tolerated for too long."[36] The influx of refugees in the streets reminded Parisians of the drama in northern France. Entire families disembarked at Gare du Nord, looking dazed. Women from the fashionable areas of Lille and Brussels arrived wearing the fur coats or minks they had hastily put on before leaving, despite the summer heat.[37]

INVASION: DEGRADATION AND DISORDER

Northern and northeastern France experienced the outbreak of war twice. The first was at the moment of the mobilization, as in the rest of France. The second was when enemy troops arrived, causing part of the population to flee. For the women, children, and elderly people left behind, the first German glimpsed at the corner of a street marked a decisive turning point. It was the beginning of the "war at home," and was accompanied by a kind of collective shock. As they headed for the front, French soldiers declared, "the Boches will not pass." Germany would be defeated by wintertime. "When the first defeats were announced, no one wanted to believe the news," remembered a schoolboy from Maretz, near Cambrai. "Anyone who dared say that we could be defeated would have been considered a traitor, a coward, a *mauvais Français*."[38]

This history of invasion and occupation has long remained unwritten, with historians' focus on combatants. Until recently, the violence experienced by civilians, including war rapes and massacres of entire villages, had also been forgotten. Especially forgotten was a German policy of occupation that we now know was a testing ground, a "laboratory," as it were, of the war violence of the twentieth century.[39]

The north and southeast of Meurthe-et-Moselle had shared borders with Germany since the war of 1870–71. This department came under enemy control the day after the declaration of war. Yet it took about three weeks for the large cities in the north of France to fall. In Valenciennes, the trams stopped on August 25. Shopkeepers closed their stores. The previous day, the mayor had signs put up, trying to avert panic. They had the opposite effect; the city was emptied of its residents within a few days. The head of the elementary school in the small village of Berlaimont in the Nord, located about eighteen miles from Valenciennes, remembered the Germans arriving: "Distraught, the curtains lowered, we witnessed the long, silent procession—gray, orderly, marked by the heavy rhythm of their hobnailed boots." A feeling of humiliation added to the initial fear. "I have to mention," wrote a teacher in Verneuil-sur-Serre in Aisne, "that their handsome appearance and their orderly, almost triumphant marching were especially painful because we had just seen our own poor exhausted soldiers painfully dragging themselves along the roads, under the burning sun."[40]

The invasion was accompanied by the destruction of many dwellings. Estimates of the number of buildings burned down by the enemy range from fifteen thousand to twenty thousand. People fleeing into the surrounding countryside returned home a few hours later, often to discover the extent of the damage. "Around 4:30, I ventured to the end of the street with my twelve-year-old son, suspicious of the smallest noise, and we did not see any Germans," recalled a teacher from Quérenaing, south of Valenciennes. "What a sight! The blaze was dying down everywhere; animals were roaming freely; through the open doors of deserted houses, we could see their interiors in shambles. The contents of cabinets had been thrown pell-mell onto the floor." Interviewed by Belgian, French, and British commissions of inquiry (the last being the famous Bryce Committee), witnesses described the shock of hearing rifle butts against their doors and seeing broken windows. They recounted being jostled and terrorized, having their mattresses ripped open. All of them associated the ransacking of their belongings with the fear of dying, which reveals the extraordinarily traumatic impact of these events.

The cities of Château-Thierry and Coulommiers were sacked. The Germans "took everything they wanted, even loading quantities of provisions and bedding onto trucks. . . . Inside the houses, they smashed whatever they did not take; I saw sizable convoys loaded up with objects which had been pillaged."[41] These acts of violence added up to much more than theft; the soldiers targeted the residents' private space itself as they soiled their bed sheets or covered the interior of their homes with excrement. "We were all terrorized," admitted a grocer from Épernay, "and even as we witnessed these depredations, we did not dare to say a single word."[42] The conquerors left an indelible imprint as they lashed out at people's homes. This desecration of domestic space, the space of conviviality and of hospitality, complicated any future return home. How could residents return when the enemy had destroyed the setting of their family memories, defiled their privacy, and obliterated any feeling of security? The violation of domestic space is similar to a "crime of desecration," targeting what is most sacred for individuals: their memories, their sense of belonging to a place and a family.[43]

Violence to spaces, violence to bodies; when they invaded Belgium and northern France at the beginning of August 1914, German soldiers were convinced that they would face the determined resistance of francs-tireurs, as in the war of 1870–71. The fear of these francs-tireurs thus preceded the war. It brought about a bloody repression that people soon started calling "German atrocities." Massacres of civilians have often been associated with the memory of the Second World War. However, in just the first few weeks of the First World War, the Germans executed more than 900 French civilians and 5,500 Belgian civilians. Women and children were separated from men, as in the Tschoffen Wall massacre in Dinant, or lined up together, without any age distinctions, as at Faubourg des Rivages on August 23, 1914.[44] In the Ardennes, 124 inhabitants of Arlon were shot in groups of ten, then "dragged by their feet and piled up, with corporals delivering a coup de grâce to those who had not yet died." Each of the five German armies invading Belgium and France participated in these atrocities at one time or another: executions, rapes, homes in ruins, pillaged churches. The American novelist Edith Wharton did humanitarian work with refugees in the north of France. In a letter to one of her friends in the

United States, she wrote: "The 'atrocities' one hears of *are true*. I know of many, alas, too well authenticated. Spread it abroad as much as you can. It should be known that it is to America's interest to help stem this hideous flood of savagery by opinion if it may not be by action. No civilized race can remain neutral in feeling now."[45]

Sexual assaults increased. They were committed at random, in the countryside, or inside houses, even in the conjugal bedroom. As soon as the war was over, in his film *J'accuse*, Abel Gance conjured up these war rapes: filmed in silhouette, the menacing faces of German soldiers wearing spiked helmets surround the young heroine Edith, who screams in terror. In regions that sheltered refugees, official police reports tell us about allegations of rape; such statements were often made in cases of pregnancy, which required that the child be given a status. The stories are all similar: soldiers erupt into the house, shouting unintelligibly in German; the victim is threatened with a weapon and forced to undress; relatives or neighbors attempt to intervene but are held back or executed. The soldier is physically strong; the rape is committed by a single aggressor, or more rarely by a group. Physical violence is inseparable from symbolic violation. For the French, the rapes expressed the unspeakable cruelty of the physical act and something else: "the anxiety of a masculinity impotent to defend the nation in its most intimate form."[46] In reality, France never recovered from the initial trauma of invasion, even after the front lines stabilized in the fall of 1914.

Then, at the end of the summer, came the enemy occupation. It enclosed the invaded regions in another temporality, different from the rest of France, which was at the time called "free France." Hanging on the smallest rumor arriving from the exterior world, occupied populations lived on German time, an hour later than French time. Reports of military operations came only via German newspapers or local gazettes, censored by the occupier. "In February 1915," recalled the head of an elementary school in Laon, "we were still unaware of the Battle of the Marne. We knew that our soldiers were ten miles south of the city, the guns thundered night and day, and every day we awaited our liberation. . . . We had no idea that trench warfare had replaced the war of movement."[47] Many inhabitants were left without news of those who had been mobilized in August 1914 or of the families that had fled at the moment of the invasion. In September, a Tourcoing housewife began a journal of the occupation, in the form of a long letter addressed to her son, a nurse in a hospital behind the front lines. She hid nothing of her difficult new life. She described her most dramatic experiences: hunger, cold, forced labor, hostages, and numerous signs of the enemy presence. Streets were given new German names, portraits of the kaiser installed in schools, and German victories on the Eastern Front saluted by ringing bells. She also related acts of resistance, like those of the parish priest of Saint-Christophe de Tourcoing, who was deported to Germany for opposing enemy requisitions. Since the war interrupted communications, her son would not read her journal until after 1918.[48]

The prospect of a short war slowly vanished. Yet it is not possible to say exactly when civilians realized that the war would be long and incredibly deadly. Public opinion had been so confident when war was first declared; what made it waver?

Was it the influx of refugees, the withdrawal of the French armies, or the first evacuations of the wounded? During the third week of August, in Côtes-du-Nord, the rumor spread that the 71st and 48th infantry regiments, garrisoned in Saint-Brieuc and in Guingamp, had suffered heavy losses. Préfets' reports from Creuse and Lozère show the same worries. The official news had only to become more laconic for the population to assume that something was being hidden from them. The préfet of Ain therefore complained about the poor functioning of the military postal service; the deaths of officers killed in action since August 9 had not been officially confirmed, but they were already being announced in the Paris newspapers.[49]

Near the end of August, news of heavy losses in the Battle of the Frontiers reached the home front. Mayors and police officers went from house to house informing the families affected. Village communities were devastated; the dead were so young, barely adults. Then the losses began to mount. More and more families felt the impact; sometimes, an entire village did. Women grew used to watching through their curtains to see where the mayor was heading on his doleful tour of bereaved households. They sighed in relief when he moved away at a bend in the road.

Other rituals also had to be created to pay tribute to the dead. Before, old peasant women in villages and nuns in the cities had known how to lay out the bodies of the dead. It was always women, the same women, who "took care of the dead." "The body has to be washed, the face shaved if it is a man, and the hair carefully combed," one of them explained. "The water used to wash the body must be thrown out far away, not down the sink or in the street. . . . When the body is ready and well dressed . . . the eyes and mouth are closed. The hands are placed on the chest and a rosary is placed on top with a sprig of boxwood blessed at the last Palm Sunday. The body is then covered with another white sheet, a nice, fine sheet."[50] All activity in the house ceased. Women neither cooked nor cleaned. The clocks were stopped. For three days, the body of the deceased was never left alone; relatives and neighbors took turns keeping vigil.

Now, after the disaster of the Battle of the Frontiers, wakes took place without a body to mourn. A series of gestures and rituals, followed to the letter from generation to generation, was brutally interrupted. Civilians could not know that soldiers' bodies had been hastily buried or left unburied. Nor could they conceive of the damage that artillery fire inflicted on these bodies. Most of the corpses were mutilated. Others had been pulverized by shells or rendered unrecognizable. None of the bodies, in any case, were returned to families, despite the requests the French population made at the end of August. Even so, people continued to gather in the houses of the deceased, quietly mourning with their neighbors. Giono described such a scene in a passage from *To the Slaughterhouse:* "Everybody from the plain was there. They had all come, the old men, the women and the little girls, and they were sitting stiffly on the stiff chairs. They said nothing. They sat on the edges of the shadows. . . . They were coming, they were all there in the farm's big room with its cold fireplace. They were there stiff and silent, keeping watch over the absent body."[51] The very experience of death and mourning had changed.

Epilogue
Beyond August 1914

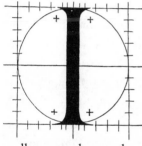 T took only a month for France to fully experience the reality of modern war. In the first ten days of the mobilization, hundreds of thousands of men were transported to the borders. There they alternated between military training and endless marches under a blazing sun. Then came the first battles. In mid-August, the French remained confident, both at the front and behind the lines. Then the situation abruptly deteriorated. In Alsace and Lorraine, offensives ended in defeat. After August 21, the situation in Hainaut and the Belgian Ardennes was a veritable disaster. The considerable human losses in Charleroi and Rossignol set a retreat in motion, as well as a general withdrawal toward Paris.

This acceleration of time was accompanied by a radical shift toward a new type of armed conflict. Military observers had described this shift during the Russo-Japanese War, but they could not imagine that one day it would materialize in Belgium and northern France. The new face of war meant weapons powerful enough to completely halt the infantry's advance, serious wounds that could not be treated, and corpses abandoned or pulverized by shelling. Civilians were now targeted. Only four days after the invasion of Belgium, 850 Belgian men, women, and children had already been executed as the German army carried out a ruthless repression of supposed francs-tireurs and their accomplices. In total, more than 6,000 were killed in two months. These numbers might seem insignificant in comparison with the atrocities of the Boer War (1899–1902) or the Balkan Wars (1912–13). But this was the first time in decades that such tragedy had unfolded in western Europe. The mass of refugees bore witness to the breadth of the disaster. On August 25, Valenciennes looked like a ghost town; three days later, Senlis and Meaux lost almost all of their inhabitants. An uncontrollable panic soon magnified the real threat of the invasion. On August 27, the city of Rouen was emptied of a third of its population, although it was far from the front. Residents had been frightened by rumors of atrocities, spread by the refugees.

August 1914 brought much suffering and disillusionment, and was felt to be an irremediable disaster. Many inhabitants of the north and northeast had lost everything. Families mourned the first deaths of the war, or anxiously awaited news of their loved ones. The wounded, in comparison, felt almost lucky. Lieutenant de Gaulle, shot in the leg on the Dinant bridge on August 15, was evacuated to Arras and then to Paris. Pierre Drieu la Rochelle, wounded in the head by shrapnel on the 23rd, was sent to the Royal Hotel in Deauville, now a makeshift hospital. André Jéramec, his best friend, was listed among the missing. As the French armies withdrew, other combatants fell into the hands of the enemy, such as Jacques Rivière, taken prisoner in Étain in the Meuse on August 24. Sent to a prison camp in Germany, a month later he found out that his brother-in-law, the young novelist Alain-Fournier, had died. The author of the classic *Le Grand Meaulnes* was killed near Saint-Rémy-la-Calonne (Meuse).

As terrible as it was, this collective ordeal was slowly forgotten. The retreat before the enemy had traumatized the French. It was almost eclipsed by the victorious counteroffensive of the Marne in early September. Then came life in the trenches, the cold, poison gas, and mass deaths in Verdun and on the Somme and on so many other battlefields. All of this made it easy to forget the rigors of the first summer of the war, especially as the conflict dragged on. More than three years passed. In the spring of 1918, Paris was once again exposed to enemy firepower. Powerful, large-caliber artillery guns, rather than a few airplanes, launched explosives. This led to numerous civilian deaths, in particular at Saint-Gervais Church on Good Friday. On May 27, 1918, the Blücher offensive was launched from the Chemin des Dames, and the Germans advanced dozens of miles. It was the dramatic episode that recalled the summer of 1914, all over again: Paris on the verge of capture. The French could feel the almost physical anguish of defeat.

But once again the Allies, supported by American soldiers and tanks, took the initiative. The breaking point was August 8, 1918. General Ludendorff later called it "the black day of the German Army in the history of this war." The Germans suffered heavy losses, including more than thirty thousand captured, according to most estimates. Over the next hundred days, the Allied armies advanced still farther, recapturing the territory taken by the enemy four years earlier. As they retreated, the Germans dynamited bridges and roads. They also burned entire villages and cut down all the fruit trees they saw. With the return to maneuver warfare, the memory of the "German atrocities" of 1914 reappeared. So did weariness, sadness, and a desire for revenge. When he discovered the atrocities committed by the enemy, a French soldier of the 117th Infantry Regiment, who had fought in the final battles around Charleville-Mézières only a few hours before the armistice, wrote in his notebook: "The Boches are finishing the war as they began it: bombing a city full of civilians with suffocating shells."[1]

On November 11, 1918, the front line passed by Maubeuge, twenty-five miles from Charleroi. Soon after the armistice, victorious French soldiers took the road through the Sambre valley. When they finally reached the old battlefield, it was no longer the same landscape as in August 1914, nor the same season. But what they saw was just as striking. Thousands of wooden crosses along the riverbanks marked the temporary graves of those who had died there four years ago. The next day, to honor the memory of their fallen comrades, soldiers in mourning decorated the crosses with the blue, white, and red of the French Republic.

Timeline

July 31
- 7 PM: Belgium declares mobilization, to begin August 1
- 9:40 PM: Jean Jaurès assassinated in a Parisian café by Raoul Villain

August 1
- 3:55 PM: General mobilization in France
- 5 PM: General mobilization in Germany
- 7 PM: Germany declares war on Russia

August 2
- Noon: First day of mobilization in France
- 10:30 AM: French corporal André Peugeot, twenty-one, becomes the first recorded fatality on the Western Front
- German Fourth Army occupies Luxembourg without opposition
- France declares a state of siege (ratified by the Law of August 5)

August 3
- 7 AM: Belgium announces that it has rejected the German ultimatum
- 6:40 PM: Germany declares war on France

August 4
- 6 AM: Germany declares war on Belgium
- 8 AM: German invasion of Belgium begins
- Burial of Jean Jaurès (afternoon)

- II PM: Protesting the violation of Belgian neutrality, Great Britain declares war on Germany

August 5

- Joffre arrives at French headquarters, established at Vitry-le-François in Champagne

August 5–16

- Battle of Liège

August 6

- Austria-Hungary declares war on Russia

August 7

- Mulhouse taken by French troops. By August 9, a larger German force pushes them back

August 7–17

- British Expeditionary Force lands in France

August 12

- France declares war on Austria-Hungary

August 13

- Germans occupy Neufchâteau in the Ardennes

August 14

- French offensive into Lorraine begins

August 15

- Lieutenant Charles de Gaulle wounded in Dinant

August 18–20

- Belgian army retreats in the direction of Antwerp

August 19

- Germans enter Louvain

August 20

- German First Army captures Brussels

August 20–24

- Battle of the Frontiers

August 20

- A massive German counterattack drives the French out of Lorraine
- French army General Pau is ordered to retreat in Alsace

August 21

- German Second Army crosses the Sambre River near Charleroi, close to the Belgian border with France. On August 23, French forces begin to withdraw to the south

August 22
- Twenty-seven thousand French soldiers killed, the bloodiest day in French military history

August 21–23
- Battle of the Ardennes; more than six hundred civilians killed, nearly ten percent of the population

August 23
- Battle of Mons

August 23
- Germans execute twenty-five Belgian civilians in Namur
- 11 PM: Lanrezac orders the 5th Army to retreat from the Sambre area

August 23–24
- German assault on Dinant

August 24
- Lille declared an open city and evacuated by French forces

August 25–26
- Destruction of the University Library of Louvain. Many summary executions of civilians

August 25–September 4
- The long Allied retreat

August 25
- Heavy fighting at Sedan between the German Fourth Army and the French 4th Army

August 26
- Gallieni becomes military governor of Paris
- Battle of Le Cateau

August 26–30
- Battle of Tannenberg in East Prussia

August 27
- General Maunoury takes command of the newly created French 6th Army
- French government reorganized; Millerand replaces Messimy as minister of war

August 28
- Retreating French 5th Army reaches the Upper Oise

TIMELINE

August 29–30
  • Battle of Guise: Lanrezac attacks the German Second Army
August 30
  • First bombing of Paris by German aircraft (afternoon)
August 31
  • A German aircraft drops leaflets on Paris announcing that the German army will arrive in three days
  • German First Army, led by von Kluck, begins to turn southeast, away from Paris. The Schlieffen Plan is falling apart
September 1
  • Von Kluck's First Army within thirty miles of Paris
September 2
  • Eugène Odent, mayor of Senlis, and six hostages are executed by German troops
  • President Poincaré and the French government leave Paris for Bordeaux (evening)
September 3
  • Paris Bourse closes
September 4
  • Ignoring orders, von Kluck pushes his First Army over the Marne (morning)
  • Joffre commits to a general counteroffensive (late afternoon)
September 6–10
  • First Battle of the Marne

Notes

INTRODUCTION

1. Bruno Cabanes, *La Victoire endeuillée. La Sortie de guerre des soldats français, 1918–1920* (Paris: Seuil, 2004); Bruno Cabanes, *The Great War and the Origins of Humanitarianism, 1918–1924* (Cambridge: Cambridge University Press, 2014).

2. Maurice Genevoix, *La Ferveur du souvenir* (Paris: Éditions de la Table Ronde, 2013), 43–45.

CHAPTER 1. WAR BREAKS OUT

1. Charles Petit-Dutaillis, *L'Appel de guerre en Dauphiné, 1er-2 août 1914* (Grenoble: Imprimerie Allier Frères, 1915).

2. Antoine Delécraz, *1914, Paris pendant la mobilisation* (Geneva: La Suisse, 1914), 13.

3. The term "président du Conseil" designates the president of the Council of Ministers, somewhat similar in rank and function to a prime minister.

4. This term refers to French citizens of every political and religious affiliation united in the common cause of defending their country.

5. Jean-Jacques Becker, *Le Carnet B* (Paris: Klincksieck, 1973).

6. Jean-Jacques Becker, *1914. Comment les Français sont entrés dans la guerre* (Paris: Presses de la Fondation nationale des Sciences Politiques, 1977), 381.

7. Henry Contamine, "Jaurès vu par les nationalistes français," *Actes du Colloque « Jaurès et la nation »* (Toulouse: Presses de la Faculté des Lettres, 1965), 123–43.

8. Archives Nationales, F7 12939, Report of the Saône-et-Loire préfet, August 2, 1914.

9. Jean Rabaut, *Jaurès et son assassin* (Paris: Éditions du Centurion, 1967).

10. This rumor is described in Delécraz, *1914*, 204.

11. Becker, *1914*, 246.

12. Ibid.

13. Jacques Droz, *Les Causes de la Première Guerre mondiale. Essai d'historiographie* (Paris: Seuil, 1973); Antoine Prost and Jay Winter, *Penser la Grande Guerre. Un essai d'historiographie* (Paris: Seuil, 2004), trans. by the authors as *The Great War in History: Debates and Controversies, 1914 to the Present* (Cambridge: Cambridge University Press, 2005).

14. Gerd Krumeich, "Pour une histoire culturelle de la décision pendant la crise de juillet 1914," in *Histoire culturelle de la Grande Guerre*, ed. Jean-Jacques Becker (Paris: Armand Colin, 2005), 239–53.

15. Pierre Renouvin, *Les Origines immédiates de la guerre, 28 juin–4 août 1914* (Paris: Alfred Costes, 1927).

16. These demands are confirmed in Adolphe Messimy's *Mes souvenirs* (Paris: Plon, 1937), 149.

17. John Keiger, *Raymond Poincaré* (Cambridge: Cambridge University Press, 1997), 170–71.

18. This telegram set in motion the concentration, that is, the deployment of troops assigned to protect the mobilization and confront initial enemy attacks.

19. Messimy, *Mes souvenirs*, 145–46.

20. Annette Becker, *Croire* (Amiens: CRDP de Picardie, 1996), 36–37.

21. Joseph Joffre, *The Personal Memoirs of Joffre, Field Marshal of the French Army*, vol. 1, trans. T. Bentley Mott (New York: Harper and Brothers, 1932), 128. Originally published as *Mémoires du Maréchal Joffre* (Paris: Plon, 1932).

22. Poincaré's diaries are kept in the manuscripts department of the Bibliothèque nationale de France, NAF 16024–27. Cited by Gerd

Krumeich, "Raymond Poincaré dans la crise de juillet 1914," in *La Politique et la Guerre. Pour comprendre le XXème siècle européen. Hommage à Jean-Jacques Becker* (Paris: Agnès Viénot, 2002), 518.

23. Delécraz, *1914*, 17.

24. Nora Bielecka, *Croquis parisiens, 1914–1918* (Paris: Éditions du "Monde" féminin, 1919), 6.

25. J. Michaux, *En marge du drame. Journal d'une Parisienne pendant la guerre, 1914–1915* (Paris: Perrin, 1916), 9.

26. Camille Clermont, *Souvenirs de Parisiennes en temps de guerre* (Paris: Berger-Levrault, 1918), 91.

27. Delécraz, *1914*, 16.

28. Daniel Halévy, *L'Europe brisée. Journal de guerre, 1914–1918* (Paris: Fallois, 1998), 29.

29. Jacques Bainville, *Journal inédit* (1914; Paris: Plon, 1953).

30. Arthur-Lévy, *1914. Août-septembre-octobre à Paris* (Paris: Plon, 1917), 24.

31. Michaux, *Journal d'une Parisienne*, 10.

32. Arthur-Lévy, *1914*, 25.

33. Delécraz, *1914*, 24.

34. Charles Ridel, *Les Embusqués* (Paris: Armand Colin, 2007).

35. Christian Mallet, *Étapes et combats. Souvenirs d'un cavalier devenu fantassin, 1914–1915* (Paris: Plon-Nourrit, 1916), 10–11.

36. Paul Hess, *La vie à Reims pendant la guerre de 1914–1918. Notes et impressions d'un bombardé* (Paris: Économica, 1998), 12.

37. Charles Berlet, *Un village lorrain pendant les mois d'août et septembre 1914* (Réméréville: Bloud et Gey éditeurs, 1916).

CHAPTER 2. VISIONS OF WAR, DREAMS OF PEACE

1. Speech delivered by de Gaulle from the Élysée and broadcast on radio and television, August 2, 1964.

2. Christopher M. Clark, *The Sleepwalkers: How Europe Went to War in 1914* (New York: HarperCollins; London: Allen Lane, 2012).

3. "La guerre," *Nouvelle Revue*, January 1, 1912, p. 66.

4. Pierre Albin, "Le risque de guerre," *La Revue de Paris*, May 1913, pp. 207–24.

5. Pierre Renouvin, *Les Origines immédiates de la guerre, 28 juin–4 août 1914* (Paris: Alfred Costes, 1927), 253.

6. Jules Isaac, *Un débat historique. 1914, le problème des origines de la guerre* (Paris: Rieder, 1933).

7. Thomas Lindemann, *Les doctrines darwiniennes et la guerre de 1914* (Paris: Économica, 2001).

8. Quoted in Stephen Kern, *The Culture of Time and Space, 1880–1918* (Cambridge: Harvard University Press, 1983), 249.

9. Emilio Gentile, *L'Apocalypse de la modernité. La Grande Guerre et l'homme nouveau* [2008], trans. S. Lanfranchi (Paris: Flammarion, 2011), 228. First published as *L'Apocalisse della modernità: la grande guerre per l'uomo nuovo* (Milan: Mondadori, 2008).

10. I. S. Bloch, *Is War Now Impossible? Being an Abridgement of "The War of the Future in Its Technical, Economic and Political Relations." With a Prefatory Conversation with the Author by W. T. Stead*, trans. W. T. Stead (London: Grant Richards, 1899), xvi.

11. Paul Louis, "La concurrence économique et les conflits internationaux," *Revue bleue*, May 16, 1914, p. 617. Quoted in Gentile, *L'apocalypse de la modernité*, 221.

12. Jean Jaurès, *L'Humanité*, May 20, 1905.

13. "I call the living, I mourn the dead and I shatter the lightning!" Jaurès quotes the epigraph to Friedrich Schiller's 1798 poem "Das Lied von der Glocke" (The song of the bell).

14. Louis Aragon, *The Bells of Basel*, trans. Haakon Chevalier (New York: Harcourt, Brace, 1936), 346. Originally published as *Les Cloches de Bâle* (Paris: Denoël et Steele, 1934), 306.

15. Gerd Krumeich, *Aufrüstung und Innenpolitik in Frankreich vor dem Ersten Weltkrieg* (Wiesbaden: F. Steiner, 1980).

16. Quoted in *July 1914: The Outbreak of the First World War: Selected Documents*, ed. and trans. Imanuel Geiss (New York: Scribner, 1967), 294–95. Original emphasis.

17. Gérard Baal, "Les débats de 1913 sur la loi des trois ans," in "Jaurès et la défense nationale," *Cahiers Jean Jaurès* 3 (1993): 110–11.

18. Patrice Mahon, "Le service de trois ans et les armements allemands," *Revue des Deux Mondes*, April 15, 1913, pp. 851–85.

19. André Tardieu, *Le Temps*, March 4, 1913.

20. Charles Péguy, *Œuvres en prose complètes* (Paris: Gallimard, Bibliothèque de la Pléiade, 1992), 3: 892.

21. Edward Berenson, *The Trial of Madame Caillaux* (Berkeley: University of California Press, 1992).

22. Roger Martin du Gard, *Les Thibault*, vol. 3, *L'Été 1914* (Paris: Gallimard, 1936), 269.

23. Agathon [Henri Massis and Alfred de Tarde], *Les Jeunes Gens d'aujourd'hui*, ed. Jean-Jacques Becker (1913; Paris: Imprimerie nationale, 1995).

24. Jean-Jacques Becker, *1914. Comment les Français sont entrés dans la guerre* (Paris: Presses de la Fondation nationale des Sciences Politiques, 1977), 62–83.

25. Ibid.

26. *Le Petit Parisien*, July 28, 1914.

27. Annie Kriegel, *Aux origines du communisme en France, 1914–1920*, 2 vols. (Paris: Mouton, 1964).

28. Rolande Trempé, *Les Mineurs de Carmaux, 1898–1914* (Paris: Éditions ouvrières, 1971), 905.

29. Louis Pergaud, letter to Jules Duboz, August 1, 1914, in *Correspondances, 1901–1915* (Paris: Mercure de France, 1955), 113.

30. Quoted in Becker, *1914*, 242 n. 307.

31. Ibid., 259–63.

32. Philippe Boulanger, *La France devant la conscription. Géographie historique d'une institution républicaine, 1914–1922* (Paris: Économica, 2001), 199–283.

33. Office universitaire de recherche socialiste, Archives Jean Texcier, 7 APO 1. Here I take up the argument developed by Romain Ducoulombier in his article "La 'Sociale' sous l'uniforme: obéissance et résistance à l'obéissance dans les rangs du socialisme et du syndicalisme français, 1914–1916," in *Obéir/ désobéir. Les mutineries de 1917 en perspective*, ed. André Loez and Nicolas Mariot (Paris: La Découverte, 2008), 266–79.

34. Raymond Poincaré, *Au service de la France*, vol. 4, *L'Union sacrée* (Paris: Plon, 1927), 546. An English translation of this particular speech was published in *Supplement to the American Journal of International Law*, vol. 9, *Official Documents* (1915): 292–93.

35. André Latreille, "1964, Réflexions sur un anniversaire," *Le Monde*, December 31, 1964.

36. Jean-Jacques Becker, "'La fleur au fusil': retour sur un mythe," in *Vrai et faux dans la Grande Guerre*, ed. Christophe Prochasson and Anne Rasmussen (Paris: La Découverte, 2004), 163.

37. Marc Bloch, *Memoirs of War, 1914–15*, trans. Carole Fink (Cambridge: Cambridge University Press, 1988), 78. First published in English by Cornell University Press, 1980. Originally published as *Souvenirs de guerre, 1914–15* (Paris: Armand Colin, 1969).

CHAPTER 3. FAREWELL CEREMONIES

1. Mark Antony de Wolfe Howe, *Memoirs of the Harvard Dead in the War against Germany* (Cambridge: Harvard University Press, 1922), 3: 229–47.

2. Leonard V. Smith, *The Embattled Self: French Soldiers' Testimony of the Great War* (Ithaca, N.Y.: Cornell University Press, 2007), 26–27.

3. According to the *New York Times* report on Herter's death, he was the first to enlist for the newly formed camouflage section. As well as his parents, he left behind a wife and two sons. "Some of the most noted artists in America were among Sergeant Herter's comrades, one of his company commanders having been Lieutenant Homer Saint-Gaudens, a son of the famous sculptor. . . . [Herter] is believed to have been wounded while camouflaging American heavy artillery on the French front. Mr. Herter, father of Sergeant Herter, has received many letters from his son in which the artist-soldier described the work he was doing on the front." *New York Times*, June 28, 1918.

4. Zacharie Baqué, *Journal d'un poilu. Août 1914-décembre 1915* (Paris: Imago, 2003), 14.

5. Louis Barthas, *Poilu: The World War I Notebooks of Corporal Louis Barthas, Barrelmaker, 1914–1918*, trans. Edward M. Strauss (New Haven: Yale University Press, 2014), 2.

6. Roland Dorgelès, *Je t'écris de la tranchée. Correspondance de guerre 1914–1917* (Paris: Albin Michel, 2003), 77.

7. Henri Barbusse, *Lettres à sa femme, 1914–1917* (Paris: Buchet-Chastel, 2006), 41.

8. L. Alexandre, *Souvenirs de la campagne 1914—Maubeuge*. Private archives, quoted in *Les Manchois dans la Grande Guerre*, ed. Patrick Fissot et al. (Marigny: Éditions Eurocibles, 2008), 34.

9. AN, F7 12937, Ariège, préfet's report, August 3, 1914.

10. AN, F7 12937, Allier, préfet's report, August 7, 1914.

11. Bruno Cabanes, *La Victoire endeuillée. La sortie de guerre des soldats français, 1918–1920* (Paris: Seuil, 2004).

12. Joseph Delteil, *Les Poilus* (Paris: Grasset, 1926).

13. Capitaine Rimbault, *Journal de campagne d'un officier de ligne* (Paris: Berger-Levrault, 1916), 19–20.

14. Ivan Cassagnau, *Ce que chaque jour fait de veuves. Journal d'un artilleur, 1914–1916* (Paris: Buchet-Chastel, 2003), 22–24.

15. Adrian Gregory, "Railway Stations: Gateways and Termini," in *Capital Cities at War: Paris, London, Berlin, 1914–1919*, vol. 2, *A Cultural History*, ed. Jay Winter and Jean-Louis Robert (Cambridge: Cambridge University Press, 2007), 23.

16. *Le Petit Journal*, August 2, 1914, p. 1.

17. Jacques Moreau, *1914–1918. Nous étions des hommes* (Paris: La Martinière, 2004), 50–51.

18. *Le Matin*, "Les femmes et la guerre," August 3, 1914, p. 1.

19. Simone de Beauvoir, *Memoirs of a Dutiful Daughter*, trans. James Kirkup (1959; New York: HarperCollins, 2005), 30. Originally published as *Mémoires d'une jeune fille rangée* (Paris: Gallimard, 1958).

20. John Horne, "*L'impôt du sang:* Republican Rhetoric and Industrial Warfare, 1914–18," *Social History* 14, no. 2 (1989): 201–23.

21. Jacques Boussac, *Correspondance de Jacques et Marie-Josèphe Boussac, 1914–1918* (Paris: Jouve, éditions familiales, 1996), 12, 16.

22. William Reddy, *The Navigation of Feeling: A Framework for the History of Emotions* (Cambridge: Cambridge University Press, 2001).

23. Jules Portes, *Souvenirs et correspondance de guerre* (Paris: Comité national, 1915), 33–34, 36.

24. Barbusse, *Lettres à sa femme, 1914–1917*, 41.

25. Dorgelès, *Je t'écris de la tranchée*, 73.

26. Martha Hanna, *Your Death Would Be Mine: Paul and Mary Pireaud in the Great War* (Cambridge: Harvard University Press, 2006).

27. Guillaume Apollinaire, *Letters to Madeleine: Tender as Memory*, trans. Donald Nicholson-Smith and ed. Laurence Campa (Chicago: University of Chicago Press, 2010), 470, letter dated December 7, 1915. See also Guillaume Apollinaire, *Calligrammes: Poems of Peace and War, 1913–1916: A Bilingual Edition*, trans. and ed. Anne Hyde Greet (Berkeley: University of California Press, 1980).

28. Maurice and Yvonne Retour, *Les Nouvelles fiançailles. Correspondance de guerre, 1914–1915* (Nantes: P. Retour, 2001), letter dated December 16, 1914, quoted by Clémentine Vidal-Naquet, "L'émotion en temps de guerre. Un couple entre séparations et retrouvailles, 1914–1915," *Traverse 2* (2007): 71.

29. Robert Hertz, *Un ethnologue dans les tranchées. Août 1914–avril 1915. Lettres de Robert Hertz à sa femme Alice* (Paris: CNRS Éditions, 2002), 99.

30. Ibid., 39.

1. Gaston Top, *Un Groupe de 75, 1e août 1914–13 mai 1915. Journal d'un médecin aide-major du 27e d'artillerie* (Paris: Plon-Nourrit, 1919), 2.

2. Henri Fauconnier, *Lettres à Madeleine, 1914–1919* (Paris: Stock, 1998), 17.

3. Damien Baldin and Emmanuel Saint-Fuscien, *Charleroi, 21–23 août 1914* (Paris: Tallandier, 2012), 29.

4. Charles de Gaulle, *Lettres, notes et carnets, 1905–1918* (Paris: Plon, 1980), 80.

5. Christian Mallet, *Étapes et combats* (Paris: Plon, 1916), 23.

6. Dr. Garret, "À la gauche du 2e R.I., carnet d'un toubib," *Revue du pays de Granville, 1929–1930*, quoted in *Les Manchois dans la Grande Guerre*, ed. Patrick Fissot et al. (Marigny: Éditions Eurocibles, 2008), 62.

7. Damien Baldin, "Les tranchées ont-elles enterré la cavalerie? Entre disparition et mutation: la cavalerie française durant la Première Guerre mondiale," *Guerres mondiales et conflits contemporains*, no. 225 (2007): pp. 7–20.

8. General M. Dragomirov, *La guerre est un mal inévitable* (Paris: H. Charles-Lavauzelle, 1897); G. F. R. Henderson, cited in Gerald French, *Good-Bye to Boot and Saddle* (London: Hutchison, 1951), 230.

9. Henri de Versonnex, *Ceux de Chamborants « sabrez ! . . . »* (Paris: Tallandier, 1933), quoted in Stéphane Audoin-Rouzeau, *Combattre. Une anthropologie historique de la guerre moderne (XIXe–XXIe siècle)* (Paris: Seuil, 2008), 267.

10. Michel Goya, *La Chair et l'acier. L'invention de la guerre moderne, 1914–1918* (Paris: Tallandier, 2004), 167–72.

11. E. L. Spears, *Liaison, 1914: A Narrative of the Great Retreat* (London: William Heinemann, 1930), 23. The frontispiece to this particular edition features a photograph not of Spears but of Joffre.

12. Louis-Ferdinand Céline, *Lettres* (Paris: Gallimard, Bibliothèque de la Pléiade, 2009), 98.

13. *Les Carnets de l'aspirant Laby, médecin dans les tranchées, 28 juillet 1914–14 juillet 1919* (Paris: Bayard, 2001), 38.

14. John Horne and Alan Kramer, *German Atrocities, 1914: A History of Denial* (New Haven: Yale University Press, 2001), 9.

15. Terence Zuber, *Inventing the Schlieffen Plan: German War Planning, 1871–1914* (Oxford: Oxford University Press, 2002).

16. Some military historians may have minimized the true consequences of von Moltke's modifications. See Martin Van Creveld, *Supplying War: Logistics from Wallenstein to Patton* (Cambridge: Cambridge University Press, 1977).

17. Horne and Kramer, *German Atrocities*, 13.

18. A franc-tireur is a guerrilla fighter. As Horne and Kramer explain, the term refers to "civilian irregular soldiers, or guerillas. . . . The term came from the Franco-Prussian War of 1870–1, when volunteer detachments of that name harassed the German armies. The image of the French franc-tireur had lingered in the German memory and imagination and re-emerged in 1914 through the belief that enemy civilians were resisting a new German invasion"; Horne and Kramer, *German Atrocities*, 1.

19. Quoted in Anne Duménil, "Le Soldat allemand de la Grande Guerre: institution militaire et expérience du combat," 2 vols., Ph.D. diss., Université de Picardie-Jules Verne, December 2000, 81 n. 128.

20. Quoted in Horne and Kramer, *German Atrocities*, 96.

21. The idea of a "beautiful death," καλός θάνατος can be traced back to ancient Greece. See Jean-Pierre Vernant, "A 'Beautiful Death' and the Disfigured Corpse in Homeric Epic," in *Mortals and Immortals: Collected Essays*, ed. Froma I. Zeitlin (Princeton: Princeton University Press, 1991).

22. Jean-Jacques Becker, *1914. Comment les Français sont entrés dans la guerre* (Paris: Presses de la Fondation nationale des Sciences Politiques, 1977), 515–23.

23. John Keegan, *The First World War* (New York: Knopf, 1999).

24. Horne and Kramer, *German Atrocities*, 56.

25. Keegan, *The First World War*.

26. Jean-Michel Steg, *Le Jour le plus meurtrier de l'histoire de France. 22 août 1914* (Paris: Fayard, 2013).

27. Georges Veaux, *En suivant nos soldats de l'Ouest* (Rennes: Imprimerie Oberthur, 1917), quoted in Baldin and Saint-Fuscien, *Charleroi*, 89–90.

28. Walter Bloem, *The Advance from Mons, 1914: The Experiences of a German Infantry Officer*, trans. G. C. Wynne (Solihull, England: Helion, 2011), 39.

29. Georges Vigarello, *Le Corps redressé* (Paris: Armand Colin, 2004).

30. John Keegan, *The Illustrated Face of Battle: A Study of Agincourt, Waterloo, and the Somme* (New York: Viking, 1988). [1976]

31. Jacques Rivière, *Carnets, 1914–1917* (Paris: Fayard, 2001), 12.

32. Maurice Genevoix, *La Mort de près* (1972; Paris: La Table ronde, 2011), 47.

33. Céline, *Lettres*, 106.

34. Maurice Genevoix, *Ceux de 14* (1950; Paris: Seuil, Points, 2013), 37.

35. De Gaulle, *Lettres, notes et carnets*, 87–88.

36. Charles Louis Marie Lanrezac, *Le Plan de campagne français et le premier mois de la guerre* (Paris: Payot, 1920), 161.

37. Baldin and Saint-Fuscien, *Charleroi*, 107.

38. *Historique du 25e Régiment d'Infanterie* (Paris: Chapelot, n.d.), 14, quoted by Fissot, *Les Manchois dans la Grande Guerre*, 69.

39. Pierre Drieu la Rochelle, *La Comédie de Charleroi* (1934; Paris: Gallimard, 1982), 86.

40. Keegan, *The Illustrated Face of Battle*.

41. Céline, *Lettres*, 98.

42. Marc Bloch, *L'Étrange Défaite* (1946; Paris: Gallimard, 1990), 86.

43. *Les Carnets de l'aspirant Laby*, 42.

44. Bloch, *L'Étrange Défaite*, 154.

45. Ian Hamilton, *A Staff Officer's Scrap-book During the Russo-Japanese War* (London: Edward Arnold, 1907).

46. M. Ferraton, "Sur les blessures de guerre par les armes modernes," *Bulletin et mémoires de la Société de chirurgie de Paris*, 1913.

47. Sophie Delaporte, *Les Médecins dans la Grande Guerre, 1914–1918* (Paris: Bayard, 2004).

48. Genevoix, *Ceux de 14*, 103.

49. Yves Desfossés, Alain Jacques, and Gilles Prilaux, *L'Archéologie de la Grande Guerre* (Rennes: Éditions Ouest-France, 2008).

50. Antoine Prost, "Compter les vivants et les morts: l'évaluation des pertes françaises de 1914–1918," *Le Mouvement social* 222 (2008): 41–60.

51. Henry Contamine, *La Victoire de la Marne, 9 septembre 1914* (Paris: Gallimard, 1970), 118–20; Baldin and Saint-Fuscien, *Charleroi*, 117.

52. Jean Galtier-Boissière, *Mémoires d'un Parisien* (Paris: La Table ronde, 1960), 129.

53. Baldin and Saint-Fuscien, *Charleroi*, 153–54.

CHAPTER 5. THE SHADOW OF DEFEAT

1. Joseph Joffre, *The Personal Memoirs of Joffre, Field Marshal of the French Army*, vol. 1, trans. T. Bentley Mott (New York: Harper and Brothers, 1932), 190. Originally published as *Mémoires du Maréchal Joffre* (Paris: Plon, 1932).

2. Hew Strachan, *The First World War*, vol. 1, *To Arms* (Oxford: Oxford University Press, 2001), 223–24.

3. Richard Cobb, "France and the Coming of War," in *The Coming of the First World War*, ed. Robert J. W. Evans and Hartmut Pogge von Strandmann (Oxford: Clarendon, 1988), 136.

4. Robert Doughty, "French Strategy in 1914: Joffre's Own," *Journal of Military History* 67, no. 2 (2003): 427–54.

5. Quoted in Fernand Gambiez and Colonel M. Suire, *Histoire de la Première Guerre mondiale* (Paris: Fayard, 1968), 1: 108.

6. Joffre, *Personal Memoirs*, 171–75.

7. Charles de Gaulle, *Lettres, notes et carnets, 1905–1918* (Paris: Plon, 1980), 94–95.

8. Gabriel Rouquerol, *Le 3ème Corps d'armée de Charleroi à la Marne. Essais de psychologie militaire. Les combattants et le commandement* (Paris: Berger-Levrault, 1934), 104.

9. Service Historique de la Défense, 26 N 107/1, 3e Corps d'armée, Artillerie, J.M.O., August 23, 1914.

10. Damien Baldin and Emmanuel Saint-Fuscien, *Charleroi, 21–23 août 1914* (Paris: Tallandier, 2012), chapter 10.

11. André Bach, *Fusillés pour l'exemple, 1914–1915* (Paris: Tallandier, 2003).

12. Jean Norton Cru, *Témoins* (Nancy: Presses Universitaires de Nancy, 1993), 367.

13. Michael Howard, "Men Against Fire: The Doctrine of the Offensive in 1914," in *Makers of Modern Strategy from Machiavelli to the Nuclear Age*, ed. Peter Paret (Princeton: Princeton University Press, 1986), 510–26.

14. Gambiez and Suire, *Histoire de la Première Guerre mondiale*, 186–87.

15. Raymond Poincaré, *Au service de la France*, vol. 5, *L'invasion* (Paris: Plon, 1927), 196.

16. SHD, 5 N 66, Telegram, August 21, 1914.

17. SHD, 1K268, Telegram from the Minister of War to Joffre, August 24, 1914, quoted by Robert A. Doughty, *Pyrrhic Victory: French Strategy and Operations in the Great War* (Cambridge: Belknap Press of Harvard University Press, 2005), 75.

18. Jean-Yves Le Naour, *Désunion nationale. La légende noire des soldats du Midi* (Paris: Vendémiaire, 2011).

19. Adolphe Messimy, *Mes souvenirs* (Paris: Plon, 1937), 374.

20. Fabienne Bock, *Un parlementarisme de guerre, 1914–1919* (Paris: Belin, 2002), 57–76.

21. Franziska Heimburger, "Une mésentente cordiale. La question des langues dans la coalition alliée pendant la Première Guerre mondiale," Ph.D. diss., l'École des Hautes Études en Sciences Sociales, 2015.

22. Joseph Gallieni, *Mémoires du maréchal Gallieni. Défense de Paris, 25 août–11 septembre 1914* (Paris: Payot, 1928), 45.

23. Walter Bloem, *The Advance from Mons, 1914: The Experiences of a German Infantry Officer*, trans. G. C. Wynne (Solihull, England: Helion, 2011).

24. Jean-Jacques Becker and Gerd Krumeich, *La Grande Guerre. Une histoire franco-allemande* (Paris: Tallandier, 2008), 199.

25. Bock, *Un Parlementarisme de Guerre*, 76.

26. Poincaré, *Au service de la France*, 5: 215–30.

27. Gallieni, *Mémoires*, 62–67.

28. Poincaré, *Au service de la France*, 5: 241.

29. Dennis E. Showalter, "Manoeuvre Warfare: The Eastern and Western Fronts, 1914–1915," in *The Oxford Illustrated History of the First World War*, ed. Hew Strachan (Oxford: Oxford University Press, 1998), 45.

CHAPTER 6. THE ENEMY WITHIN

1. Michael Jeismann, *Das Vaterland der Feinde. Studien zum nationalen Feindbegriff und Selbstverständnis in Deutschland und Frankreich, 1792–1918* (Stuttgart: Klett-Cotta, 1992).

2. Antoine Delécraz, *1914, Paris pendant la mobilisation* (Geneva: La Suisse, 1914), 98–99.

3. Gundula Bavendamm, *Spionage und Verrat. Konspirative Kriegserzählungen und französische Innenpolitik, 1914–1917* (Essen: Klartext, 2003), 52–70.

4. Pierre Renouvin, *Les Formes du gouvernement de guerre* (Paris: Presses universitaires de France; New Haven: Yale University Press, 1925).

5. Henri Plait, *L'État de siège et la restriction des libertés individuelles pendant la guerre 1914–1919* (Auxerre: Imprimerie Maurice Staub, 1920), 30–31.

6. Aladár Kuncz, *Le Monastère noir* (Paris: Gallimard, 1937), 15.

7. Jean Signorel, *Le Statut des sujets ennemis* (Paris: Berger-Levrault, 1916), 25.

8. AN, 12988, Morbihan, préfet's report, August 5, 1914.

9. Archives départementales, Côtes-d'Armor, 9 R 7, quoted in Jean-Claude Farcy, *Les camps de concentration français de la Première Guerre mondiale, 1914–1920* (Paris: Anthropos, 1995), 12.

10. Archives de la Préfecture de Police de Paris, archives de la main courante, CB 36.31, 36ème commissariat de police du quartier Rochechouart, No. 706, August 27, 1914.

11. APPP, archives de la main courante, CB 53.18, 53ème commissariat de police du quartier de Montparnasse, No. 731, August 12, 1914.

12. Ibid., No. 750, August 17, 1914.

13. APPP, archives de la main courante, CB 57.38, 57e commissariat de police du quartier Saint-Lambert, No. 1114, August 6, 1914.

14. Farcy, *Les camps de concentration français*, 12.

15. AN, F7 12938, Haute-Marne, préfet's report, August 3, 1914.

16. AN, F7 12938, Hautes-Pyrénées, préfet's report, August 3, 1914.

17. Farcy, *Les Camps de concentration français*, 37.

18. Patrick Weil, *Qu'est-ce qu'un Français? Histoire de la nationalité française depuis la Révolution* (Paris: Grasset, 2002), 70.

19. Manon Pignot, *Paris dans la Grande Guerre* (Paris: Éditions Parigramme, 2014), 20.

20. "Faut-il encore apprendre l'allemand?" *L'Action française*, October 10, 1914, p. 1.

21. Gabriel Veraldy, *Le Roman d'espionnage* (Paris: PUF, 1983).

22. Alain Dewerpe, *Espions. Une anthropologie historique du secret d'État contemporain* (Paris: Gallimard, 1994), 298.

23. Ibid., chapter 8, "Les scandales de la révélation."

24. Paul Lanoir, *The German Spy System in France* (London: Mills and Boon, 1910), 231–33. Originally published as *L'Espionnage allemand en France. Son organisation, ses dangers, les remèdes nécessaires* (Paris: Publications littéraires illustrées, Cocuaud et Cie, 1908).

25. APPP, archives de la main courante, CB 39.67, 39e commissariat de police du quartier de la Porte Saint-Martin, Nos. 965, 966 and 967, August 13, 1914.

26. AN, F7 12 938, Berlaimont gendarmerie, Nord département, August 14, 1914.

27. Ibid., Meuse, préfet's report to the minister of the interior, August 5, 1914.

28. AN, F7 12 939, Saône-et-Loire, préfet's report to the minister of the interior, August 8, 1914.

29. APPP, archives de la main courante, CB 24.26, 24e commissariat de police du quartier Saint-Germain des Prés, No. 505, August 15, 1914.

30. Delécraz, *1914*, 125–26.

31. Dewerpe, *Espions*.

32. Délécraz, *1914*, 99.

33. AN, F7 12938, Rhône, préfet's report to the minister of the interior, August 13–14, 1914.

34. APPP, BA 889, Guerre de 1914—lumières, signaux suspects.

35. Robert Wohl, *A Passion for Wings: Aviation and the Western Imagination, 1908–1918* (New Haven: Yale University Press, 1994), 69–94.

36. Susan Grayzel, *At Home and Under Fire: Air Raids and Culture in Britain from the Great War to the Blitz* (Cambridge: Cambridge University Press, 2012).

37. Tami Davis Biddle, "Air Power," in *The Laws of War: Constraints on Warfare in the Western World*, ed. Michael Howard et al. (New Haven: Yale University Press, 1994), 140–59.

38. Susan Grayzel, "The Souls of Soldiers: Civilians Under Fire in First World War France," *Journal of Modern History*, 78, no. 3 (2006): 588–622.

39. "Bombs Dropped in Paris," *The Times*, August 31, 1914; "The Paris Bombs," *The Times*, September 4, 1914.

40. Vanessa Schwartz, *Spectacular Realities: Early Mass-Culture in Fin-de-Siècle Paris* (Berkeley: University of California Press, 1998).

41. Jules Poirier, *Les Bombardements de Paris, 1914–1918* (Paris: Payot, 1930), 95–96.

42. Simone Delattre, *"Les Douze Heures noires." La nuit à Paris au XIXème siècle* (Paris: Albin Michel, 2000).

43. APPP, BA 889, Guerre de 1914—lumières, signaux suspects; Letter dated September 4, 1914, to the préfet de police de Paris. Original emphasis.

44. APPP, BA 889, Guerre de 1914—lumières, signaux suspects; Letter dated September 6, 1914, to the commissariat de police du quartier de la Madeleine.

45. Eugen Weber, *Action française: Royalism and Reaction in Twentieth-Century France* (Stanford: Stanford University Press, 1962), 89–90.

46. Léon Daudet, *L'Avant-guerre. Études et documents sur l'espionnage juif-allemand en France depuis l'affaire Dreyfus* (Paris: Nouvelle Librairie nationale, 1913), viii.

47. *L'Action française*, July 31, 1914, p. 1.

48. *L'Action française*, July 30, 1914, p. 1.

49. Weil, *Qu'est-ce qu'un Français?* 63.

50. Rapport du comité de législation de la Chancellerie, May 1915, quoted ibid., 70.

51. Signorel, *Le Statut des sujets ennemis*, chap. 2.

52. Daudet, *L'Avant-guerre*, 5–6.

53. Delécraz, *1914*, 99–100.

CHAPTER 7. FEARS AND RUMORS

1. Marc Bloch, "Reflections of a Historian on the False News of the War," trans. James P. Holoka, *Michigan War Studies Review*, July 2013, http://www.miwsr.com/2013-051.aspx. Originally published as "Réflexions sur les fausses nouvelles de la guerre," *Revue de synthèse historique* 33 (1921); rpt. in Marc Bloch, *L'Histoire, la Guerre, la Résistance* (Paris: Gallimard, collection Quarto, 2006).

2. For example, Antoine Delécraz, *1914, Paris pendant la mobilisation* (Geneva: La Suisse, 1914); Albert Dauzat, *Légendes, prophéties et superstitions de la Grande Guerre* (Paris, 1919); Arthur Ponsonby, *Falsehood in War-Time: Containing an Assortment of Lies Circulated Throughout the Nations During the Great War* (New York: Dutton, 1928).

3. Delécraz, *1914*, 28–32.

4. Lucien Graux, *Les Fausses nouvelles de la Grande Guerre* (Paris: L'édition française illustrée, 1918–20), 365.

5. Georges Ohnet, *Journal d'un bourgeois de Paris pendant la guerre de 1914* (Paris: Librairie Paul Ollendorff, 1914), 20.

6. John Horne and Alan Kramer, *German Atrocities, 1914: A History of Denial* (New Haven: Yale University Press, 2001).

7. Ibid.

8. Sophie Huet, *Quand ils faisaient la guerre* (Paris: Plon, 1993), 15, quoted in Philippe Nivet, *Les Réfugiés français de la Grande Guerre. Les « Boches du Nord »* (Paris: Économica, 2004), 26.

9. Madame Emmanuel Colombel, *Journal d'une infirmière d'Arras* (Paris: Bloud et Gay, 1916), 32.

10. Nivet, *Les Réfugiés français de la Grande Guerre*, 27.

11. Raoul de Navery, *Madeleine Miller, histoire alsacienne* (Paris, 1878), 162.

12. Horne and Kramer, *German Atrocities*, 183 ff.

13. Marcel Proust, *Le Temps retrouvé* (1927; Paris: Garnier-Flammarion, 1986), 120; trans. as *In Search of Lost Time: Finding Time Again*, Ian Patterson (London: Penguin, 2002), 58.

14. AN, F7 12937, préfet's report, Ain, August 22, 1914.

15. AN, F7 12939, préfet's report, Tarn et Garonne, August 26, 1914.

16. AN, F7 12938, préfet's report, Oise, August 26, 1914.

17. AN, F7 12937, préfet's report, Corrèze, August 24, 1914.

18. Horne and Kramer, *German Atrocities*.

19. *Les Enfants dans la Grande Guerre*, catalogue d'exposition, Historial de Péronne, 2003, p. 17.

20. Les livres roses pour la jeunesse, 1917, No. 202, 23, quoted in Stéphane Audoin-Rouzeau, *La Guerre des enfants, 1914–1918* (Paris: Armand Colin, 1993), 142–43.

21. Ibid., 236–42.

22. *Le Matin*, September 20, 1914.

23. Gabriel Boitelle, *Mes souvenirs de la Grande Guerre*, quoted in Manon Pignot, *Allons enfants de la patrie. Génération Grande Guerre* (Paris: Seuil, 2012), 46.

24. Viscount James Bryce, *Report of the Committee on Alleged German Outrages* (London, 1915).

25. André Gide, *The Journals of André Gide*, trans. Justin O'Brien (New York: Knopf, 1948), 92. Originally published as *Journal, 1889–1939* (Paris: Gallimard, 1939), 500–501. Entry dated November 15, 1914.

26. Pignot, *Allons enfants de la patrie*, 44–48.

27. Michael Teitelbaum and Jay Winter, *The Fear of Population Decline* (Orlando: Academic Press, 1985).

28. AN, F7 12938, préfet's report, Lozère, August 15, 1914.

29. *L'Express du midi*, August 13, 1914, p. 1.

30. AN, F7 12938, préfet's report, Lot-et-Garonne, August 9, 1914.

31. Dauzat, *Légendes, prophéties et superstitions de la Grande Guerre*, 55–56.

32. Delécraz, *1914*, 49.

33. Nicolas Delbaere, "La trajectoire de la Société laitière Maggi dans la dynamique du transport du lait en France durant la première moitié du XXème siècle: du bidon à la gare laitière," *Revue d'histoire des chemins de fer* 41 (2010): 205–20.

34. APPP, archives de la main courante, CB 53.18, 53ème commissariat de police du quartier de Montparnasse, no. 712, August 3, 1914.

35. *L'Action française*, August 3, 1914.

36. AN, F7 12939, préfet's report, Seine-et-Marne, August 4, 1914, in the morning. The same day, two men were arrested on the avenue d'Orléans in Paris, because they were smashing down a newsstand that had a Maggi poster. APPP, archives de la main courante, CB 54.23, 54ème et 55ème commissariats de police du quartier de la Santé et de Petit-Montrouge, No. 694, August 4, 1914.

37. AN, F7 12936, rapport du préfet de Seine-et-Oise, August 3, 1914.

38. Jean-Jacques Becker, *1914. Comment les Français sont entrés dans la guerre* (Paris: Presses de la Fondation nationale des Sciences Politiques, 1977), 498.

39. *Le Petit Marseillais*, August 5, 1914.

40. Delécraz, *1914*, 59, 73-75.

41. *La Guerre sociale*, August 6, 1914.

42. Delécraz, *1914*, 78.

43. APPP, archives de la main courante, CB 24.26, 24ème commissariat de police du quartier Saint-Germain des Prés, no. 487, August 3, 1914.

44. APPP, archives de la main courante, CB 50.25, 50ème commissariat de police du quartier de la Gare, no. 895, August 3, 1914.

45. Jean-Noël Jeanneney, *Jours de guerre 1914-1918. Les trésors des archives photographiques du journal « Excelsior »* (Paris: Les Arènes, 2014), 38-39.

CHAPTER 8. THE SOUNDS OF WAR

1. Antoine Delécraz, *1914, Paris pendant la mobilisation* (Geneva: La Suisse, 1914), 107.

2. Jean Giono, *To the Slaughterhouse*, trans. Norman Glass (London: Peter Owen, 1969), 18. Original published as *Le Grand Troupeau* (1931; Paris: Gallimard, 1997), 24.

3. Yvonne Verdier, *Façons de dire, façons de faire. La laveuse, la couturière, la cuisinière* (Paris: Gallimard, 1979), 338-39.

4. Michel Augé-Laribé, *L'Agriculture pendant la guerre* (Paris: Presses universitaires de France; New Haven: Yale University Press, 1925), 66-67.

5. AN, F7 12 939, préfet's report, Tarn-et-Garonne, August 14, 1914.

6. Colette, *Les Heures longues, 1914-1917* (Paris: Fayard, 1917), 174-75.

7. AN, F7 12 938, préfet's report, Manche, August 8, 1914.

8. AN, F7 12 939, préfet's report, Seine-et-Marne, August 2, 1914.

9. AN, F7 12 938, préfet's report, Hautes-Pyrénées, August 8, 1914.

10. Augé-Laribé, *L'Agriculture pendant la guerre*, 119.

11. Patrick Fissot et al., eds., *Les Manchois dans la Grande Guerre* (Marigny: Éditions Eurocibles, 2008), 99.

12. H. Person, *Derrière les tranchées* (Neuilly-sur-Seine, n.d.), 7. Quoted in Gene Tempest, "The Long Face of War: Horses in the French and British Armies on the Western Front," Ph.D. diss., Yale University, 2013, p. 46.

13. SHD, 7N451, Instruction du 22 décembre 1898 sur la réquisition des animaux et voitures de complément nécessaires à l'armée en cas de mobilisation, mise à jour le 20 mars 1913 (Instruction dated December 22, 1898, concerning the requisition of supplemental animals and cars needed by the army in case of mobilization, updated March 20, 1913).

14. SHD, 16 N 2543, circulaire fixant le prix des chevaux de réquisition, April 18, 1913.

15. Charles Petit-Dutaillis, *L'Appel de guerre en Dauphiné, 1er–2 août 1914* (Grenoble: Imprimerie Allier Frères, 1915), 56–57.

16. SHD, 7N451, "Instruction du 22 décembre 1898 sur la réquisition des animaux et voitures."

17. Eric Baratay, *Bêtes de tranchées. Des vécus oubliés* (Paris: CNRS Éditions, 2013), 24–25.

18. SHD, 7N459. See Tempest, *The Long Face of War,* 44.

19. SHD, 7N 451, quoted in Tempest, *The Long Face of War,* 62.

20. Giono, *To the Slaughterhouse,* 97–98 (*Le Grand Troupeau,* 122).

21. Jules Poirier, *Les Bombardements de Paris, 1914–1918* (Paris: Payot, 1930).

22. Mathieu Flonneau, *Paris et l'automobile. Un siècle de passions* (Paris: Hachette, 2005), 92.

23. Fernand Laudet, *Paris pendant la guerre, impressions* (Paris: Perrin, 1915), 32.

24. Anonymous, *L'Âme de Paris,* 1915, pp. 1–3.

25. Pierre Barral, *Les Agrariens français de Méline à Pisani* (Paris: Armand Colin, 1968), 179–80.

26. John Horne, "*L'impôt du sang:* Republican Rhetoric and Industrial Warfare in France, 1914–1918," *Social History* 14, no. 2 (1989): 201–23.

27. Arthur Fontaine, *L'Industrie pendant la guerre* (Paris: Presses universitaires de France; New Haven: Yale University Press, 1924), 51.

28. Henri Sellier, A. Bruggeman and Marcel Poëte, *Paris pendant la guerre* (Paris: Presses universitaires de France; New Haven: Yale University Press, 1926), 8–9.

29. Laudet, *Paris pendant la guerre*, 30.

30. Ibid.

31. APPP, D/B 343, dépêche du préfet de police Hennion, August 15, 1914.

32. Emmanuelle Cronier, "The Street," in *Capital Cities at War: Paris-London-Berlin, 1914–1919*, ed. Jay Winter and Jean-Louis Robert (Cambridge: Cambridge University Press, 2002), 2: 61.

33. Jean-Yves Le Naour, *Misères et tourments de la chair pendant la Grande Guerre* (Paris: Aubier-Montaigne, 2002).

34. Anonymous, *L'Âme de Paris*, 1–3.

35. *Excelsior*, August 5, 1914, quoted in Delécraz, *1914*, 87. "Modern style" in English in the original.

36. *La Croix*, September 1, 1914.

37. André Gunthert, ed., *Paris 14–18. La guerre au quotidien* (Paris: Paris bibliothèques, 2014).

38. Réponses au questionnaire adressé par le recteur de l'académie de Lille sur l'occupation du Nord de la France, 1920, Fonds de la Bibliothèque de documentation internationale contemporaine, Nanterre.

39. Annette Becker, *Les cicatrices rouges. 14–18. France et Belgique occupées* (Paris: Fayard, 2010).

40. Réponses au questionnaire adressé par le recteur de l'académie de Lille.

41. AN, AJ4 5, deposition of François Bétancourt, deputy mayor of Château-Thierry, December 11, 1914. Quoted in John Horne and Alan Kramer, *German Atrocities, 1914: A History of Denial* (New Haven: Yale University Press, 2001).

42. AN, 4AJ19, testimony of Mme Rainguet, quoted in John Horne, "Corps, lieux et nation: La France et l'invasion de 1914," *Annales. Histoire, Sciences Sociales* 55, no. 1, (2000): 73–109, quotation from 91.

43. Véronique Nahoum-Grappe, "The Anthropology of Extreme Violence: The Crime of Desecration," *International Social Science Journal* 54, no. 174 (2002), 549–57.

44. Horne and Kramer, *German Atrocities.*

45. Letter to Sara Norton, September 2, 1914, in Edith Wharton, *The Letters of Edith Wharton,* ed. R. W. B. Lewis and Nancy Lewis (New York: Scribner, 1988), 335; emphasis original.

46. Horne, "Corps, lieux et nation," 95.

47. Réponses au questionnaire adressé par le recteur de l'académie de Lille.

48. Annette Becker, *Oubliés de la Grande Guerre. Humanitaire et culture de guerre. Populations occupées, déportés civils, prisonniers de guerre* (Paris: Noésis, 1998), 29.

49. AN, F7 12937, préfet's report (Ain) to the minister of the interior, August 29, 1914.

50. Verdier, *Façons de dire, façons de faire,* 101.

51. Giono, *To the Slaughterhouse,* 62 (*Le Grand Troupeau,* 81–82).

EPILOGUE

1. Bruno Cabanes, *La Victoire endeuillée. La Sortie de guerre des soldats français, 1918–1920* (Paris: Seuil, 2004), 68.

Index